Collins
COBUILD

Key Words for
Retail

HarperCollins Publishers
Westerhill Road
Bishopbriggs
Glasgow
G64 2QT

First Edition 2013

Reprint 10 9 8 7 6 5 4 3 2 1 0

© HarperCollins Publishers 2013

ISBN 978-0-00-749028-8

Collins® and COBUILD® are
registered trademarks of
HarperCollins Publishers Limited

www.collinslanguage.com

A catalogue record for this book is
available from the British Library

CD recorded by Networks SRL,
Milan, Italy

Typeset by Davidson Publishing
Solutions, Glasgow

Printed in Great Britain by Clays Ltd,
St Ives plc

Acknowledgements
We would like to thank those authors
and publishers who kindly gave
permission for copyright material
to be used in the Collins Corpus.
We would also like to thank Times
Newspapers Ltd for providing
valuable data.

Contents

Contributors

Specialist consultant
Val Shields, Retail Analyst, Strategic Marketing Manager

Project manager
Patrick White

Editors
Katherine Carroll
Kay Cullen
Janice McNeillie
Enid Pearsons
Elizabeth Walter
Kate Woodford

Computing support
Mark Taylor

For the publisher
Gerry Breslin
Lucy Cooper
Kerry Ferguson
Gavin Gray
Elaine Higgleton
Persephone Lock
Ruth O'Donovan
Rosie Pearce
Lisa Sutherland

Introduction

Collins COBUILD Key Words for Retail is a brand-new vocabulary book for students who want to master the English of Retail in order to study or work in the field. This title contains the 500 most important English words and phrases relating to Retail, as well as a range of additional features which have been specially designed to help you to *really* understand and use the language of this specific area.

The main body of the book contains alphabetically organized dictionary-style entries for the key words and phrases of Retail. These vocabulary items have been specially chosen to fully prepare you for the type of language that you will need in this field. Many are specialized terms that are very specific to this profession and area of study. Others are more common or general words and phrases that are often used in the context of Retail.

Each word and phrase is explained clearly and precisely, in English that is easy to understand. In addition, each entry is illustrated with examples taken from the Collins Corpus. Of course, you will also find grammatical information about the way that the words and phrases behave.

In amongst the alphabetically organized entries, you will find valuable word-building features that will help you gain a better understanding of this area of English. For example, some features provide extra help with tricky pronunciations, while others pull together groups of related words that can usefully be learned as a set.

At the start of this book you will see lists of words and phrases, helpfully organized by topic area. You can use these lists to revise sets of vocabulary and to prepare for writing tasks. You will also find with this book an MP3 CD, containing a recording of each headword in the book, followed by an example sentence. This will help you to learn and remember pronunciations of words and phrases. Furthermore, the exercise section at the end of this book gives you an opportunity to memorize important words and phrases, to assess what you have learned, and to work out which areas still need attention.

So whether you are studying Retail, or you are already working in the field and intend to improve your career prospects, we are confident that *Collins COBUILD Key Words for Retail* will equip you for success in the future.

Guide to Dictionary Entries

Headwords are organized in alphabetical order

Pronunciation

Subject areas are highlighted and link the word to the thematic word lists

Synonyms help expand your vocabulary

Word classes are shown for every word

Information boxes help expand your vocabulary and increase your understanding of the word and when to use it

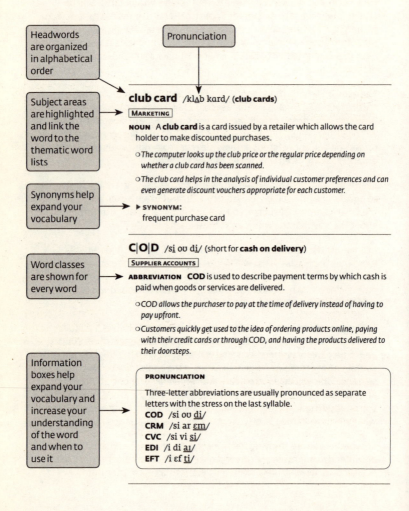

club card /klʌb kɑrd/ (**club cards**)

| MARKETING |

NOUN A **club card** is a card issued by a retailer which allows the card holder to make discounted purchases.

○ *The computer looks up the club price or the regular price depending on whether a club card has been scanned.*

○ *The club card helps in the analysis of individual customer preferences and can even generate discount vouchers appropriate for each customer.*

▶ **SYNONYM:**
 frequent purchase card

C|O|D /si oʊ di/ (short for **cash on delivery**)

| SUPPLIER ACCOUNTS |

ABBREVIATION **COD** is used to describe payment terms by which cash is paid when goods or services are delivered.

○ *COD allows the purchaser to pay at the time of delivery instead of having to pay upfront.*

○ *Customers quickly get used to the idea of ordering products online, paying with their credit cards or through COD, and having the products delivered to their doorsteps.*

PRONUNCIATION

Three-letter abbreviations are usually pronounced as separate letters with the stress on the last syllable.
COD /si oʊ di/
CRM /si ar ɛm/
CVC /si vi si/
EDI /i di aɪ/
EFT /i ɛf ti/

Guide to Dictionary Entries

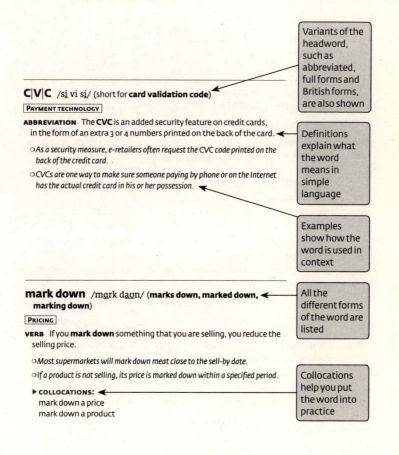

C|V|C /si vi si/ (short for **card validation code**)

PAYMENT TECHNOLOGY

ABBREVIATION The **CVC** is an added security feature on credit cards, in the form of an extra 3 or 4 numbers printed on the back of the card.

○ *As a security measure, e-retailers often request the CVC code printed on the back of the credit card.*

○ *CVCs are one way to make sure someone paying by phone or on the Internet has the actual credit card in his or her possession.*

mark down /mɑrk daun/ (**marks down, marked down, marking down**)

PRICING

VERB If you **mark down** something that you are selling, you reduce the selling price.

○ *Most supermarkets will mark down meat close to the sell-by date.*

○ *If a product is not selling, its price is marked down within a specified period.*

▸ **COLLOCATIONS:**
mark down a price
mark down a product

Variants of the headword, such as abbreviated, full forms and British forms, are also shown

Definitions explain what the word means in simple language

Examples show how the word is used in context

All the different forms of the word are listed

Collocations help you put the word into practice

Guide to Pronunciation Symbols

Vowel Sounds

ɑ	calm, ah
ɑr	heart, far
æ	act, mass
ɑɪ	dive, cry
ɑɪər	fire, tire
aʊ	out, down
aʊər	flour, sour
ɛ	met, lend, pen
eɪ	say, weight
ɛər	fair, care
ɪ	fit, win
i	feed, me
ɪər	near, beard
ɒ	lot, spot
oʊ	note, coat
ɔ	claw, bought
ɔr	more, cord
ɔɪ	boy, joint
ʊ	could, stood
u	you, use
ʊər	lure, endure
ɜr	turn, third
ʌ	fund, must
ə	*the first vowel in* about
ər	*the first vowel in* forgotten
i	*the second vowel in* very
u	*the second vowel in* actual

Consonant Sounds

b	bed, rub
d	done, red
f	fit, if
g	good, dog
h	hat, horse
y	yellow, you
k	king, pick
l	lip, bill
ᵊl	handle, panel
m	mat, ram
n	not, tin
ᵊn	hidden, written
p	pay, lip
r	run, read
s	soon, bus
t	talk, bet
v	van, love
w	win, wool
ʍ	why, wheat
z	zoo, buzz
ʃ	ship, wish
ʒ	measure, leisure
ŋ	sing, working
tʃ	cheap, witch
θ	thin, myth
ð	then, other
dʒ	joy, bridge

Word Lists

CUSTOMER ACCOUNTS
account
budget account
cash
cash discount
cash receipt
cash up
change
charge
charge account
chargeback
check
check guarantee
check verification
credit
employee discount
float
installment
installment plan
installment sales
merchant account
merchant fees
merchant service
on account
on credit
payment
petty cash
quantity discount
receipt
refund
store credit
take
takings

DISTRIBUTION
back order
bonded warehouse
carrier
consignment
deliver
delivery
distribution
drop-ship
drop shipment
export
FOB
forwarding agent
fulfillment
home delivery
import

just-in-time
JV
logistics
mail order
minimum order
packing slip
pallet
palletize
procurement
RTV
ship
shipment
shipper
shipping documents
supplier
supply chain

GENERAL
at wholesale
chamber of commerce
checkout line
e-commerce
in-store
loss prevention
m-commerce
merchantable
order
overstock
purchase
retail
return
sale
serial number
shopping bag
soft sell
store rollout
traffic
vend
walk-in traffic
wholesale

MANAGEMENT ACCOUNTS
accounts payable
accounts receivable
commission
FIFO
general ledger
gross
gross profit
gross profit margin

inventory adjustment
inventory cost
journal
LIFO
like-for-like
lossmaker
lossmaking
net
proceeds
processor
profit
profit center
profit margin
receivables
return on investment
revenue
reversal
sales tax
standard cost
tax
tax refund
trading period
transaction
turnover
turn over
undercharge
unit cost

MARKETING
BOGO
brand
bundle
club card
comparison shopping
CRM
customer data
customer experience
customer flow
customer preference
customer profile
fascia
frequent shopper program
frontage
lifestyle
livery
loyalty
loyalty card
market
marketable
market data

market research
mystery shopper
niche
niche market
own brand
own label
point of sale
pre-sell
promotion
promotional code
promotional event
QR code
retail analytics
sales forecast
seasonal promotion
signage
store front
store launch event
tearsheet
USP
value
VIC
voucher

MERCHANDISING
available quantity
beginning inventory
bulk buying
carry
clearance
destock
display
ending inventory
fire sale
flash sale
in stock
inventory
merchandise
merchandising
model stock
move
offer
on hand
on order
on-shelf
out of stock
overage
overbuy
overstock
periodic inventory

perpetual inventory
physical inventory
pick
picking ticket
purchase request
replenish
replenishment
rotating stock
sale
saleable
sell off
sell out
sell-through
short order
shrinkage
SKU
spot lighting
stock
stock allocation
stocking unit
stock order
stockroom
stocktaking
stock transfer
underbuy
vendible
visual merchandising
VMI
warehouse
window display
window dressing

OUTLETS

big-box
boutique
bricks and mortar
cash-and-carry
catchment area
chain
chain store
clicks and mortar
concession
convenience store
department store
destination store
discount store
emporium
e-tail
factory outlet
flagship store

food court
franchise
grocer
hypermarket
independent
kiosk
leisure retail
location
Main Street
market
marketplace
mart
mom-and-pop store
multiple store
outlet
out-of-town
pop-up
premises
retail anchor
shop
shop-in-shop
shopping center
shopping mall
showroom
sideline
small-format
store
strip-mall
supermarket
superstore
value retailer
vending machine
vertical retailer
virtual retail
warehouse

PAYMENT TECHNOLOGY

address verification service
approval code
authorization
barcode
barcode reader
cash register
CVC
EDI
EFT
EFTPOS
electronic receipt
encryption
e-payment

EPOS
MSR
PIN
point-of-sale terminal
PVV
scanner
UPC

PERSONNEL
buyer
buying manager
cashier
category merchandiser
category planner
distributor
floorwalker
intern
junior sales associate
merchant
operations manager
personal shopper
sales associate
sales clerk
sales manager
sales representative
security guard
security manager
shopkeeper
storekeeper
store manager
trader
tradesman
tradespeople
vendor
window dresser

PRICING
cut-price
discount
list price
loss leader
margin
markdown
mark down
markup
mark up
MSRP
offer
off-price
on sale

overcharge
pay-per-click
predatory pricing
price
price break
price check
price comparison
price-fixing
price-sensitive
price tag
price war
pricing gun
resale price maintenance
retail price
RRP
undercut
underprice
unit price

PRODUCTS
accessories
apparel
assortment
babywear
back catalogue
bespoke
catalogue
category
category listing
childrenswear
couture
custom-made
designer clothing
electronics
firsts
FMCG
footwear
goods
haberdashery
hardware
home entertainment
household goods
housewares
interiors
item
lighting
line
merchandise
multipack
non-food

nursery
on the market
order
pack
package
packaging
perishables
product
range
ready-to-wear
sample
season
seasonal
seconds
selection
sell-by date
sell in
soft furnishings
thirds
top-of-the-line
unit
use-by date

SERVICE
aftercare
B2B
B2C
call center
client
custom
customer
customer-facing
customer service
customer support
gift card
gift certificate
gift receipt
giftwrap
gift-wrap
gratis
guarantee
patron
sale or return
sales commission
sales pitch
sales slip
special order
warranty

STORE FIXTURES AND LAYOUT
bargain basement
bargain bin
bin
checkout counter
corner rack
cube unit
department
display case
end cap
fitting room
fixture
garment rack
gondola
grid merchandiser
gridwall panel
hanger
hang tag
kit
mannequin
retail theater
RFID tag
self-checkout
shelving unit
shop floor
signposting
slatwall merchandiser
slatwall panel
storage unit
store refurbishment
tag
ticket

SUPPLIER ACCOUNTS
back-dated
bill
bill of lading
COD
cost
dun
duty
duty-free
invoice
on consignment
pro forma invoice
purchase order
receiver
tender
terms
trade discount

A–Z

Aa

ac|ces|so|ries /æksɛsəriz/

PRODUCTS

NOUN **Accessories** belong to a product category in fashion stores, which includes items such as scarves, hats, gloves, belts, and purses.

- ○ *Retail sales of both men's and women's fashion accessories finished the year on an up note, with hats and scarves the bestselling products.*
- ○ *The company manufactures bridal accessories, including veils, gloves, and hair ornaments.*

ac|count /əkaʊnt/ (accounts)

CUSTOMER ACCOUNTS

NOUN An **account** is a regular client or customer, such as a firm or trader buying goods or supplies on credit.

- ○ *New account applications require information to be filled out first by the potential customer, then by the company for quotation, and then back to the customer for final signature.*
- ○ *We have gained some new clients to offset the old clients, but we've probably lost more accounts than we've gained.*

ac|counts pay|a|ble (ABBR **AP**) /əkaʊnts peɪəbᵊl/

MANAGEMENT ACCOUNTS

NOUN A company's **accounts payable** are all the money that it owes to other companies for goods or services that it has received, or a list of these companies and the amounts owed to them.

- ○ *On the liabilities side, the accounts payable to suppliers, wages payable to employees, and taxes payable are current liabilities.*
- ○ *Because every dollar you have in accounts payable is a dollar added to cash, it is a vital part of a financial analysis.*

A

> **WORD BUILDER**
> **-able/-ible** = able to be done
>
> The suffixes **-able** and **-ible** often appear in adjectives that mean that a particular thing can be done to something: **accounts receivable**, **marketable**, **merchantable**, **saleable**, **vendible**.

---

ac|counts re|ceiv|a|ble (ABBR **AR**) /əkaunts rɪsiːvəbəl/

`MANAGEMENT ACCOUNTS`

NOUN A company's **accounts receivable** are all the money that it is owed by other companies for goods or services that it has supplied, or a list of these companies and the amounts that they owe.

○ Unpaid bills from other companies, or trade credit, make up the bulk of accounts receivable.

○ Most business-to-business transactions involve sales on credit, usually 30-day terms, and that leads to accounts receivable.

---

ad|dress ver|i|fi|ca|tion ser|vice (ABBR **AVS**) /ədrɛs vɛrɪfɪkeɪʃən sɜːvɪs/ (**address verification services**)

`PAYMENT TECHNOLOGY`

NOUN **Address verification service** is a system which, in order to limit credit card fraud, permits merchants to electronically check a buyer's billing address against the credit card holder's address to see if they match.

○ Address verification service reduces credit card fraud by verifying the cardholder's address information when the physical card isn't available to swipe through an MSR device.

○ Unfortunately, address verification services only really work for US cardholders, leaving foreign card transactions at risk of fraud.

---

af|ter|care /æftərkɛər/

`SERVICE`

NOUN **Aftercare** is any system of maintenance offered with a product or appliance.

○ The aftercare offered with the computer is excellent, especially the dedicated helpline.

○ *The quality of the aftercare (by a service visit or helpdesk, for example) may be as important a factor as price in the purchase decision.*

---

ap|par|el /əpǽrəl/

PRODUCTS

NOUN **Apparel** is a general name for various types of clothing.

○ *They are an apparel retailer that offers clothing, shoes, and accessories for men, women, and children.*

○ *They specialize in the supply of sports apparel such as sweatshirts and baseball caps to retail markets.*

---

ap|prov|al code /əprúvəl koʊd/ (**approval codes**)

PAYMENT TECHNOLOGY

NOUN An **approval code** is a PIN or other verification code needed to authorize a payment going through the cash register.

○ *An approval code, typically consisting of numbers, is given when a credit card transaction is authorized.*

○ *The approval code is a six-digit alphanumeric code assigned by the card issuer to identify the approval for a specific authorization request.*

▶ **SYNONYM:**
   authorization code

---

as|sort|ment /əsɔ́rtmənt/ (**assortments**)

PRODUCTS

NOUN The **assortment** of goods in a store is the selection of varied merchandise it stocks.

○ *A store may order part of its assortment on a weekly basis, while another part is ordered on a daily basis.*

○ *A retailer's assortment is defined by the set of products carried in each store at each point in time.*

---

at whole|sale /æt hoʊlseɪl/

GENERAL

PHRASE Goods bought and sold **at wholesale** are bought and sold in large quantities at cost price or wholesale price.

○ *Even the best discount value will not be as good as buying the item at wholesale.*

○ *These are the companies that claim they supply at wholesale, but the discount is so minimal you can find it cheaper on the Internet.*

▶ **COLLOCATIONS:**
buy at wholesale
sell at wholesale

---

au|thor|i|za|tion /ɔθərɪzeɪʃən/

Payment technology

NOUN **Authorization** is the process of checking that a card holder has enough credit before funds are released to make a payment.

○ *The order goes through a series of steps, including a risk check to see whether the order appears fraudulent, and a credit card authorization.*

○ *Point-of-sale staff must follow standard authorization procedures when a customer pays by credit card.*

---

a|vail|a|ble quan|ti|ty /əveɪləbəl kwɒntɪti/ (available quantities)

Merchandising

NOUN The **available quantity** of a product is the amount of that product available, or currently available in the store.

○ *Generally, the available quantity is equal to the on-hand quantity minus any quantities set aside for open orders.*

○ *The available quantity is the quantity of an item that is currently available for sale.*

Bb

B|2|B /biː tə biː/ (short for **business to business**)

`SERVICE`

ABBREVIATION **B2B** is trade between commercial organizations rather than between businesses and private customers.

○ *Manufacturers, wholesalers, and suppliers are typical B2B companies.*

○ *The retail exchange enables retailers to interact with other retailers for B2B transactions.*

B|2|C /biː tə siː/ (short for **business to consumer**)

`SERVICE`

ABBREVIATION **B2C** is trade between businesses and consumers, often via the Internet.

○ *Retailers are typical B2C companies.*

○ *The B2C business model focuses on sales to consumers.*

---

ba|by|wear /beɪbiwɛər/

`PRODUCTS`

NOUN **Babywear** is a clothing product category for babies and infants up to 2 years old.

○ *Sales of babywear were worth about $5 million last year, with Babygros the bestselling item.*

○ *It is one of the few remaining manufacturers of babywear and childrenswear in the country.*

> **RELATED WORDS**
>
> Compare **babywear** with **childrenswear** which is a clothing product category for children under 12.

B

back cat|a|logue (or **back catalog**) /bæk kætəlɒg/ (**back catalogues**)

PRODUCTS

NOUN A company's **back catalogue** is a list of the products it offered for sale in the past.

○ A back catalogue of shoes that are considered "classics" adds to brand equity.

○ We have a back catalogue of 35 offers which are no longer available to new customers but which existing customers may still be enjoying.

back-dat|ed /bækdeɪtɪd/

SUPPLIER ACCOUNTS

ADJECTIVE If a purchase order or invoice is **back-dated**, it is given a date that is some time before the date it was actually prepared.

○ A back-dated invoice may have been created for legitimate accounting reasons, but, even so, it should be queried.

○ It appears that the invoice has been back-dated with the intention of misleading the Customs Department.

back or|der /bæk ɔrdər/ (**back orders**)

DISTRIBUTION

NOUN A **back order** is created when there is not enough of a product available to fill a current sale or order.

○ Demand has been greater than anticipated and the number of back orders is increasing steadily.

○ Back orders for out-of-stock products may be handled in several ways including cancellation, product substitution, and sourcing from alternate distribution facilities in the network.

bar|code (or **bar code**) /bɑrkoʊd/ (**barcodes**)

PAYMENT TECHNOLOGY

NOUN A **barcode** is a unique series of parallel lines printed on a product's packaging, which is scanned to register its price at the checkout, and to manage stock.

○ Barcodes give retailers a better way to track inventory, help reduce labor costs, and enhance the overall customer shopping experience.

○ *Each item has its barcode scanned to determine its expiration date and condition.*

OTHER BARCODES

The following are also types of code used in product tracking and payment:

QR code
a code containing information about an item, such as a description and the price, made up of a pattern of black squares or dots, which can be read and processed by a cellphone

RFID tag
a barcode that makes use of radio waves to send information tracking individual products at every stage, from delivery to stockroom to checkout, in a networked system

---

bar|code read|er /bɑ̱rkoʊd ri̱dər/ (**barcode readers**)

STORE FIXTURES AND LAYOUT
PAYMENT TECHNOLOGY

NOUN A **barcode reader** is an electronic scanning machine that reads and sends barcode information.

○ *There are three kinds of barcode readers: the handheld reader, the fixed mount reader, and the reader gates.*

○ *Some grocery retailers have smartphone applications including a barcode reader, which allows customers to scan barcodes of grocery products and add them to their online orders.*

▶ **SYNONYM:**
barcode scanner

---

bar|gain base|ment /bɑ̱rgɪn be̱ɪsmənt/ (**bargain basements**)

STORE FIXTURES AND LAYOUT

NOUN A department store with a **bargain basement** has an area or floor below the first floor where goods are sold at reduced prices.

○ *In our oldest store, we also have our popular bargain basement, where goods and apparel are sold at reduced or discounted prices.*

○ *As a rule, the bargain basement will have an item in only one or two sizes or styles, at heavily discounted prices.*

B

bar|gain bin /bɑ̱rgɪn bɪn/ (**bargain bins**)

STORE FIXTURES AND LAYOUT

NOUN A **bargain bin** is a container in a store where old or damaged goods are offered for sale at reduced prices.

○ As well as the full-price high-end ranges of shoes, there will also be a bargain bin with shoes priced at $25.

○ The bargain bin was full of cut-price slow-moving stock.

be|gin|ning in|ven|to|ry /bɪgɪnɪŋ ɪnvᵊntɔri/ (**beginning inventories**)

MERCHANDISING

NOUN A **beginning inventory** is all of the goods, services, or materials that a business has available for use or sale at the start of a new accounting period.

○ If the beginning inventory is overstated, cost of goods sold will be overstated and net income understated.

○ The cost of the ending inventory is larger than the cost of the beginning inventory because the firm bought more than it sold.

be|spoke (also known as **custom-made**) /bɪspoʊk/

PRODUCTS

ADJECTIVE **Bespoke** items are designed or made to fit the requirements of an individual customer.

○ The company offers a bespoke, "tailor made" vacation service to Australia, New Zealand, Africa, and Asia.

○ The men's clothing boutique is a combination of designer and bespoke merchandise.

▶ **COLLOCATIONS:**
bespoke product
bespoke service

big-box /bɪg bɒks/

OUTLETS

ADJECTIVE **Big-box** stores are very large retail stores, often part of a chain.

○ *Smaller retailers may be able to compete with big-box stores and other mega-retailers by concentrating on agility, adaptability, customer service, and credibility.*

○ *Large-scale retail formats are often referred to as big-box retailers.*

▶ **COLLOCATIONS:**
bigbox retailer
bigbox store

---

bill¹ /bɪl/ (bills)

SUPPLIER ACCOUNTS

NOUN A **bill** is a request for payment by a seller for goods or services provided.

○ *The company could no longer afford to pay their bills.*

○ *If any violation of the shipping instructions causes an increase in shipping charges paid by the retailer, the resulting increased charge will be deducted from the bill.*

---

bill² /bɪl/ (bills, billed, billing)

SUPPLIER ACCOUNTS

VERB If you **bill** someone **for** goods or services, you send them a bill stating how much money they owe you.

○ *Are you going to bill me for this?*

○ *The company billed us for storage of items that have been out of the company's hands for three months.*

---

bill of lad|ing /bɪl əv leɪdɪŋ/ (bills of lading)

SUPPLIER ACCOUNTS

NOUN A **bill of lading** is a document containing full details of goods that are being shipped.

○ *The bill of lading is issued by the carrier, and shows that the carrier has originated the shipment of merchandise.*

○ *The bill of lading is forwarded to the importer for the goods to be released.*

B

bin /bɪn/ (**bins**)

STORE FIXTURES AND LAYOUT

NOUN A **bin** is an area within a larger division of the warehouse or stockroom. Bins are numbered or coded so that stock may be checked and found easily.

○ *This less formal display method sees product being "dumped" into the display bin rather than being stacked in an orderly fashion.*

○ *The label tells the warehouse staff which bin the goods are to be stored in.*

BO|GO (in BRIT use **BOGOF**) /ˈboʊgoʊ/

MARKETING

ABBREVIATION **BOGO** is a way of encouraging more sales of a product by offering customers another item of the same type, free or for a reduced price. The UK variant stands for "buy one, get one free."

○ *The store's BOGO offers dominated their promotional activities.*

○ *Many customers are in the habit of buying only BOGO offers, regardless of the brand, because of the great value.*

> **PRONUNCIATION**
>
> Note that this abbreviation is pronounced as a single word rather than as individual letters. The following abbreviations are also pronounced as words:
> **EFTPOS** /ˈɛftpɒs/
> **EPOS** /ˈipɒs/
> **FIFO** /ˈfaɪfoʊ/
> **LIFO** /ˈlaɪfoʊ/
> **PIN** /pɪn/
> **SKU** /skyu/

bond|ed ware|house /ˈbɒndɪd ˈwɛərhaʊs/ (**bonded warehouses**)

DISTRIBUTION

NOUN A **bonded warehouse** is a secure warehouse in which goods are stored until customs duty is paid or the goods are cleared for export.

○ *Authorized operators of bonded warehouses are often required to provide custom bond.*

○ *The bottled Scotch is stored in a bonded warehouse until all the customs' formalities have been completed.*

---

bou|tique /butik/ (boutiques)

OUTLETS

NOUN A **boutique** is a small retail store selling fashionable clothes, gifts, and accessories.

○ *She launched her first boutique selling her own designs after taking a fashion course in Paris.*

○ *These designer fashions are available only in the most exclusive boutiques and high-end outlets.*

---

brand /brænd/ (brands)

MARKETING

NOUN A **brand** is a name, trademark, or other symbol which distinguishes a product or manufacturer from others in the market, for example Coca Cola, Apple, or Ford.

○ *The company's objective is to become the leading Internet-based music media company and to create a global brand.*

○ *Goods at the mid to low end of the market have reported poor sales in recent trading statements, while luxury brands are still turning huge profits.*

> **Talking about brands**
>
> If a store **carries** or **stocks** a particular brand, it offers it for sale.
>
> A **leading**, **best-selling**, or **top-selling** brand is one of the most popular brands.
>
> An **exclusive**, **luxury**, or **premium** brand is a very expensive brand.
>
> A brand **identity** or **image** is the way that people think of a particular brand, for example whether they think it is expensive, good quality, or stylish, etc.

B

bricks and mor|tar /brɪks ənd mɔrtər/

OUTLETS

ADJECTIVE A **bricks and mortar** retail business is one that has one or more premises that customers may shop in, rather than one that does business only online.

○ The company's Web presence replicates the bricks and mortar experience of its customers.

○ Many companies saw the advent of online retailing as a threat to their bricks and mortar business.

budg|et ac|count /bʌdʒɪt əkaʊnt/ (budget accounts)

CUSTOMER ACCOUNTS

NOUN A **budget account** is a customer account with a retailer that allows the customer to make regular monthly payments to cover past and future purchases.

○ A budget account may be linked to a credit card, allowing the card holder to buy an expensive item over a longer period of time.

○ Many department stores offer their customers budget accounts to encourage sales of bigger ticket items.

bulk buy|ing /bʌlk baɪɪŋ/

MERCHANDISING

NOUN **Bulk buying** is the buying at one time of a large quantity of a particular product.

○ Most of our customers want small quantities, but the option of bulk buying is also available, for which delivery on time is assured.

○ Bulk buying, movement and storage brings in economies of scale, thus savings in inventory.

bun|dle /bʌndəl/ (bundles, bundled, bundling)

MARKETING

VERB If you **bundle** one product with another to attract business, you give away a relatively cheap item to customers when you sell them a more expensive one.

○ *Sellers often bundle several of their products at a reduced price.*

○ *Own-brand shampoo and conditioner has been bundled and further discounted with a BOGO offer.*

buy|er /baɪər/ (buyers)

PERSONNEL

NOUN A **buyer** is an employee whose job is to buy products and materials, for example to stock a store or supply a factory.

○ *Our senior buyers are responsible for various buying roles in homewares, household appliances, and seasonal categories such as Christmas and Easter.*

○ *At the trade show buyers from the largest retail chains are wined and dined by manufacturers and suppliers.*

buy|ing man|ag|er /baɪɪŋ mænɪdʒər/ (buying managers)

PERSONNEL

NOUN The **buying manager** of a store is a senior employee whose job is to manage the purchase and delivery of products and supplies, maintaining stock levels.

○ *Buying managers can easily review, evaluate, and manipulate each purchase order by looking forward in time, or by selectively increasing specific line items to reduce freight costs.*

○ *The responsibilities of a buying manager can include ordering, vendor negotiations, and delivery chasing.*

Cc

---

call cen|ter (BRIT call centre) /kɔl sɛntər/ (call centers)

SERVICE

NOUN A **call center** is a customer service center where employees of a company deal with inquiries, handle technical support, or take sales, via the telephone.

○ The call center handles customer service as well as retail sales, billing, and collection.

○ Many companies are now choosing to repatriate their customer service call centers and set them up in the US.

---

car|ri|er /kæriər/ (carriers)

DISTRIBUTION

NOUN A **carrier** is any business that transports goods from the seller to the buyer, by road, air, train, or ship.

○ If shipping cartons are damaged, the carrier should note this on the delivery receipt.

○ The delivery can be tracked online, showing which depot the carrier last delivered the goods to, and when.

---

car|ry /kæri/ (carries, carried, carrying)

MERCHANDISING

VERB If a store **carries** a certain product or category of product, it offers it for sale.

○ The company carried a wide assortment of industrial products from ladders and generators to mops and cleaning supplies.

○ A typical store may carry up to 12,000 items and a megastore 50,000 items.

cash /kæʃ/

CUSTOMER ACCOUNTS

NOUN **Cash** is money in the form of bills and coins.

○ *Are you paying by cash, check, or card?*

○ *They paid us $2000 in cash.*

C

cash-and-car|ry /kæʃ ənd kæri/ (cash-and-carries)

OUTLETS

NOUN A **cash-and-carry** is a self-service wholesale store, especially for groceries, at which customers pay at each visit and take the goods they have bought away with them.

○ *Warehouse clubs are large-scale, members-only establishments that combine features of cash-and-carry wholesaling with discount retailing.*

○ *Cash-and-carries serve the needs of small retailers which use them just as a consumer uses a supermarket.*

cash dis|count /kæʃ dɪskaʊnt/ (cash discounts)

CUSTOMER ACCOUNTS

NOUN A **cash discount** is a reduction in price that is given to a purchaser who pays in cash or before a particular date.

○ *Are you prepared to offer a cash discount for prompt payment?*

○ *Goods may be sold on terms which allow the customer a cash discount of 8 percent if the bill is paid within 10 days of the end of month.*

cash|ier /kæʃɪr/ (cashiers)

PERSONNEL

NOUN A **cashier** is a person who customers pay money to or get money from in a store.

○ *The cashier said that my card had been refused.*

○ *The head cashier counts the contents of all the till drawers in the store and completes a daily bank deposit slip.*

C

cash re|ceipt /kæʃ rɪsit/ (**cash receipts**)

CUSTOMER ACCOUNTS

NOUN A **cash receipt** is a proof of purchase issued when the buyer has paid in cash.

○ *This cash receipt form is perfect for any industry and can be provided as proof of payment, or payment received.*

○ *Cash receipts are the printed documents which are issued each and every time cash is received for a specific service or good.*

cash reg|is|ter /kæʃ rɛdʒɪstər/ (**cash registers**)

PAYMENT TECHNOLOGY

NOUN A **cash register** is a machine on which sales are rung up and recorded, usually with a drawer containing money for use in making change for customers who pay in cash.

○ *If the sale is by cash or check, the cashier rings it up on the cash register and gives change.*

○ *By adding the beginning cash to the daily sales figure, a retailer will know exactly how much money should be in the cash register at any given time.*

cash up /kæʃ ʌp/ (**cashes up, cashed up, cashing up**)

CUSTOMER ACCOUNTS

VERB When cashiers and storekeepers **cash up**, they add up all the money taken from customers during a shift, or at the end of the working day.

○ *Cashing up involves calculating and saving the expected contents of the till and resetting it ready for the next session.*

○ *When cashing up, the cash drawer and its contents should be taken to an office or other secluded area.*

cat|a|logue (or **catalog**) /kætˀlɒg/ (**catalogues**)

PRODUCTS

NOUN A **catalogue** is a book or magazine containing details and pictures of items currently being offered for sale, especially as used by companies that do much of their business by mail order.

○ *Catalogues usually come out every January during the summer and spring season, with another coming out in July for the fall and winter season.*

○Virtual retailing has the advantage of linking inventory with the website and an online catalogue that the customer can browse.

---

catch|ment ar|e|a /kætʃmənt ɛəriə/ (**catchment areas**)

OUTLETS

NOUN A store's **catchment area** is the area surrounding it from which consumers are likely to travel to shop at the store.

○Stores can be clustered and managed depending on their catchment area.

○The company always does advance research on the demographic profile of any proposed new store's catchment area.

---

cat|e|go|ry /kætɪgɔri/ (**categories**)

PRODUCTS

NOUN A **category** in retailing is a grouping of the same or similar products such as breakfast cereals, soft drinks, or detergents.

○Presentation will be a key factor in merchandising impulse categories such as apparel, home fashions, and perishables.

○Technology and social media was found to have an increasingly important role in selling to 18–30 year olds in two categories: fashion and grocery.

---

cat|e|go|ry list|ing /kætɪgɔri lɪstɪŋ/ (**category listings**)

PRODUCTS

NOUN A **category listing** is a list of different product categories such as menswear, womenswear, and childrenswear.

○Dynamic category listing software allows you to create and utilize any type of category easily on a retailing website.

○The new category listings on the site reflect the retailer's expansion into new product lines.

---

cat|e|go|ry mer|chan|dis|er /kætɪgɔri mɜrtʃəndaɪzər/ (**category merchandisers**)

PERSONNEL

NOUN A **category merchandiser** is a person whose job is to maintain stocks, manage displays and promote sales of a certain product category such as footwear.

○ The category merchandiser makes final decisions about what to purchase.

○ Suppliers' sales reps deal with the category merchandiser or the store buyer for a particular department.

---

cat|e|go|ry plan|ner /kætɪgɔri plænər/ (**category planners**)

PERSONNEL

NOUN A **category planner** is a person whose job to plan and co-ordinate future inventory and sales volume in one or more product categories.

○ The category planner's role is managing the demand and supply requirements for customers across various business units.

○ The category planner has responsibility for an entire product line.

---

chain /tʃeɪn/ (**chains**)

OUTLETS

NOUN A **chain** is a number of similar stores, hotels or restaurants with the same owner or management.

○ They are a nationwide retail chain with over 90 stores.

○ Large retail chains have pushed out many of the independent businesses from town centers.

> **RELATED WORDS**
>
> A retailer that is not part of one of the big retail **chains** is described as **independent**.
>
> ○ The big chains have driven a lot of smaller, independent retailers out of business.

---

chain store /tʃeɪn stɔr/ (**chain stores**)

OUTLETS

NOUN A **chain store** is one of a group of stores engaged in the same kind of business in different locations and under the same ownership and management.

○ Chain stores in malls or shopping centers are always looking to improve their position and strengthen their brand identity in the marketplace.

○ *While it is true that smaller stores cannot generally compete strictly on price with the large chain stores, they can still compete.*

cham|ber of com|merce /tʃeɪmbər əv kɒmɜːrs/ (chambers of commerce)

GENERAL

NOUN The **chamber of commerce** in a town, city or area is an organization made up of local business people to promote, regulate, and protect their interests.

○ *The local chamber of commerce can also provide vendor and supplier connections to entrepreneurs just starting out.*

○ *The US Chamber of Commerce has members ranging from mom-and-pop stores to leading industry associations and large corporations.*

change /tʃeɪndʒ/

CUSTOMER ACCOUNTS

NOUN **Change** is the amount of money handed back to a customer when they have paid with bills or coins that total more than the amount due.

○ *The sales clerk gave her change for a $10 bill.*

○ *The sales clerk gave the customer her change and put her purchases in a bag.*

charge /tʃɑːrdʒ/ (charges, charged, charging)

CUSTOMER ACCOUNTS

VERB If you **charge** someone, you ask them to pay an amount of money for something that you have sold to them or done for them.

○ *The 4 percent tax is charged on any item that costs less than $110.*

○ *The consultant charged us a fee of $7500.*

charge ac|count /tʃɑːrdʒ əkaʊnt/ (charge accounts)

CUSTOMER ACCOUNTS

NOUN A **charge account** is an arrangement where a customer can purchase products or services on credit.

○ *Charge accounts mean that you can still buy when you are short of cash, and take advantage of sales and bargains.*

○ *Many customers take advantage of our charge accounts at times of heavy expenditure, such as Christmas.*

---

charge|back /tʃɑ̱rdʒbæk/ (chargebacks)

CUSTOMER ACCOUNTS

COUNT/NONCOUNT NOUN A **chargeback** is the act of charging a cost back to an account.

○ *If someone has paid money into the account and not received the goods, under what is called a chargeback, the company can take money from the seller's account and return it to the buyer.*

○ *Assuming you paid by credit card, the best way to get a refund is to reclaim the money via a chargeback.*

---

check (BRIT cheque) /tʃɛ̱k/ (checks)

CUSTOMER ACCOUNTS

NOUN A **check** is a printed form from a bank that you write on and use to pay for things, your bank then paying the money from your account.

○ *He paid me with a check for $1,500.*

○ *The card will guarantee checks up to $500.*

---

check guar|an|tee (BRIT cheque guarantee) /tʃɛ̱k gæ̱rənti/ (check guarantees)

CUSTOMER ACCOUNTS

NOUN A **check guarantee** is any method, usually via a plastic card, that guarantees that a payment made by check will be honored by the account holder's bank.

○ *Check guarantee will guarantee a customer's payment by check, up to a specified amount.*

○ *Most check guarantees only cover amounts up to two or three hundred dollars.*

---

check|out coun|ter (in BRIT use cash desk) /tʃɛ̱kaʊt kaʊntər/ (checkout counters)

STORE FIXTURES AND LAYOUT

NOUN A **checkout counter** is a place in a store where customers go to pay for the goods they want to buy.

○ *Customers scan the items being purchased at a checkout counter, pay electronically by credit or debit card, and bag the items themselves.*

○ *Grocery stores' checkout counters generally have conveyor belts to move the goods along.*

C

check|out line /tʃɛkaʊt laɪn/ (checkout lines)

GENERAL

NOUN A **checkout line** is a line of customers waiting to pay at a checkout counter.

○ *A policy that more and more stores are implementing is to have one single checkout line, divided into several checkout counters at the end.*

○ *Checkout lines can get very long at busy times.*

check ver|i|fi|ca|tion (Brit cheque verification) /tʃɛk vɛrɪfɪkeɪʃ°n/

CUSTOMER ACCOUNTS

NOUN **Check verification** is a system that checks national databases of information about individuals to make sure that checks will be honored and fraud is not being committed.

○ *The credit agency offers a check verification service for merchants, designed to expedite the processing and handling of checks and reduce fraud.*

○ *Check verification isn't possible across international borders, so it makes sense to insist on travelers' checks or some other form of payment.*

chil|drens|wear /tʃɪldrənz wɛər/

PRODUCTS

NOUN **Childrenswear** is a clothing product category for children under 12.

○ *They have broadened their childrenswear offer with new designer ranges for boys and girls.*

○ *Fashion saw a five percent increase on the same period, thanks to strong sales in back-to-school childrenswear and womenswear.*

C

clear|ance /klɪərəns/ (clearances)

MERCHANDISING

NOUN **Clearance** is the selling of merchandise, at greatly reduced prices, often to make way for new stock.

○ *The retailer was closing its stores and so was holding a clearance sale.*

○ *The store had a clearance sale to reduce its inventory of slow-moving stock.*

clicks and mor|tar /klɪks ənd mɔrtər/

OUTLETS

ADJECTIVE A **clicks and mortar** business is one that combines traditional trading methods with Internet trading.

○ *The so-called clicks and mortar approach creates a mutually beneficial relationship between the physical presence many existing companies have and their online outlets.*

○ *A clicks and mortar strategy converts traditional physical inventory to an advantage by harnessing it with online catalog access.*

cli|ent /klaɪənt/ (clients)

SERVICE

NOUN A **client** is a customer.

○ *They not only aim to sell goods but also they take pride in how they serve their clients.*

○ *The checkout staff must always treat every client with the utmost politeness.*

▶ **SYNONYM:**
customer

club card /klʌb kɑrd/ (club cards)

MARKETING

NOUN A **club card** is a card issued by a retailer which allows the card holder to make discounted purchases.

○ *The computer looks up the club price or the regular price depending on whether a club card has been scanned.*

○ *The club card helps in the analysis of individual customer preferences and can even generate discount vouchers appropriate for each customer.*

▶ SYNONYM:
frequent purchase card

C|O|D /siː oʊ diː/ (short for **cash on delivery**)

SUPPLIER ACCOUNTS

ABBREVIATION COD is used to describe payment terms by which cash is paid when goods or services are delivered.

○ COD allows the purchaser to pay at the time of delivery instead of having to pay upfront.

○ Customers quickly get used to the idea of ordering products online, paying with their credit cards or through COD, and having the products delivered to their doorsteps.

> **PRONUNCIATION**
>
> Three-letter abbreviations are usually pronounced as separate letters with the stress on the last syllable.
> **COD** /si oʊ diː/
> **CRM** /si ar ɛm/
> **CVC** /si vi siː/
> **EDI** /i di aɪ/
> **EFT** /i ɛf tiː/

---

com|mis|sion /kəmɪʃᵊn/

MANAGEMENT ACCOUNTS

NOUN Commission is payment of part of the revenues or profits from a sale or deal that is paid to the person who arranged or facilitated the deal.

○ Travel agents charge 1 percent commission on tickets.

○ The salespeople work on commission only.

▶ COLLOCATION:
commission on

---

com|par|i|son shop|ping /kəmpærɪsən ʃɒpɪŋ/

MARKETING

NOUN Comparison shopping is comparing similar products from different stores or suppliers. Comparison shopping services are popular on the Internet.

○ *Comparison shopping should be done by all retailers to find out what their competition is doing in regards to pricing, merchandising, store layouts, staffing, and new products.*

○ *The use of comparison shopping websites to find the best prices has become widespread.*

---

con|ces|sion[1] /kənsɛʃ°n/ (concessions)

OUTLETS

NOUN An individual or business operating a **concession** within another business's premises has been granted a license to run a subsidiary business on those premises.

○ *A local butcher operates a concession in the large general food store.*

○ *The company won the concession for 7 new stores at the airport.*

---

con|ces|sion[2] /kənsɛʃ°n/ (concessions)

OUTLETS

NOUN In a department store, a **concession** is a business with a license or contract to operate another business within the store.

○ *The company is an established concession in a busy mid-market ladies fashion retailer at the local mall.*

○ *The retailer has 26 stores, concessions in 15 department stores, and a presence in 8 stores through other partnerships.*

---

con|sign|ment /kənsaɪnmənt/

DISTRIBUTION

NOUN **Consignment** is the act of leaving goods with someone else to sell while retaining ownership until the goods are sold.

○ *Goods are sometimes supplied on a consignment basis, so that payment is not made until after the buyer has sold the goods, and in the meantime the goods remain the property of the supplier.*

○ *When a manufacturer supplies goods to a dealer on consignment, the dealer can return the goods without incurring a loss.*

con|ven|i|ence store /kənvinyəns stɔr/ (**convenience stores**)

OUTLETS

NOUN A **convenience store** is a small, local, easily accessed store which stocks staples such as bread and milk, and packaged foods.

○ *As more gas stations become fully fledged convenience stores, shoppers are also expecting to see a well-managed range of fresh and chilled foods.*

○ *There is still a place for local convenience stores in a retail landscape dominated by big-box retailers.*

> **RELATED WORDS**
>
> Compare **convenience store** with **mom-and-pop store** which is also a small retail store but one that is owned and operated by members of the same family.

cor|ner rack /kɔrnər ræk/ (**corner racks**)

STORE FIXTURES AND LAYOUT

NOUN A **corner rack** is a shelving unit designed to fit into corners to maximize space.

○ *The products were displayed on a corner rack in the far corner of the store, behind the checkout.*

○ *Corner racks make good use of those awkward corners and are especially easy to restock.*

cost¹ /kɔst/ (**costs**)

SUPPLIER ACCOUNTS

NOUN The **cost** of an item is the amount the buyer has to pay the seller for it.

○ *The cost for the replacement items was $2,200.*

○ *The cost as advertised was more than he was prepared to pay.*

cost² /kɔst/ (**costs, costed, costing**)

SUPPLIER ACCOUNTS

VERB When you **cost** an item or a process, you calculate its cost to you or how much it will cost over its lifetime.

C

○ *Having costed the likely loss of business that complete closure would cause, the manager decided to keep the store open while repairs went on.*

○ *The less experienced retailer may neglect to cost everything in their business plan.*

---

cou|ture /kutʊər/

PRODUCTS

NOUN **Couture** is high-fashion clothing for women.

○ *If you compare it with a ready-to-wear garment, you will see immediately that a couture version of the same garment is better.*

○ *The dress designer specializes in making elegant couture bridal and evening wear at her exclusive showroom.*

---

cred|it¹ /krɛdɪt/ (credits)

CUSTOMER ACCOUNTS

NOUN If a store or supplier issues a **credit** to a customer, they give the customer a sum of money or equivalent purchasing power to spend at a later date.

○ *An exchange or replacement may be provided to the purchaser if it is available, and refunds or credits will be provided for returned items in most cases.*

○ *Any credits for returned items should show up on your account within 24 hours.*

---

cred|it² /krɛdɪt/

CUSTOMER ACCOUNTS

NOUN If a person or business buys on **credit**, the seller allows the buyer to receive goods or services before making payment.

○ *Net income is adjusted for any sales or expenditures made on credit and not yet paid with cash.*

○ *Set-up costs will be minimized if suppliers allow you to buy fixtures and fittings on credit.*

C|R|M /si ɑr ɛm/ (short for **customer relationship management**)

MARKETING

ABBREVIATION **CRM** is the mix of strategies used by a company to deal with existing customers, or to attract new customers.

○ CRM is vital to the marketing people our sales representatives call on every day.

○ These new CRM products help with strategies to build customer loyalty and address the issue of tying marketing to sales revenue objectives.

---

cube u|nit /kyu̱b yunɪt/ (cube units)

STORE FIXTURES AND LAYOUT

NOUN **Cube units** are shelving units made up of horizontal and vertical dividers which form open-ended cubes, suitable for displaying products such as towels in a range of colors.

○ Cashmere sweaters and scarves in a wide range of colors are displayed in perspex cube units.

○ Cube units are versatile, being stackable and providing a dual view of the merchandise.

---

cus|tom¹ /kʌstəm/

SERVICE

NOUN If you give a store or business your **custom**, you buy from them.

○ Shoppers are extremely loyal to their regular newspaper and you risk losing their custom for good if it is not available.

○ He said he was dissatisfied with the service and would be taking his custom elsewhere.

---

cus|tom² /kʌstəm/

SERVICE

NOUN A store or business's **custom** is all its customers.

○ Custom has fallen off over the years as people move to the suburbs.

○ Creating a pedestrian area will generate more custom for the stores and restaurants in the street.

---

cus|tom|er /kʌstəmər/ (customers)

SERVICE

NOUN A **customer** is someone who buys products or services.

○ He introduced stricter measures for slow-paying customers and directed his sales staff to find new accounts.

C

○ *The store design leads customers through each department, with the aim of maximizing impulse buying.*

▶ SYNONYM:
client

Talking about customers

Potential or **prospective** customers are people who may be customers for a particular store in the future.

A store's customer **base** is the group of people who buy products from that store, and **existing** customers are people who already regularly buy products from the store.

Customer **satisfaction** is when customers are pleased with the products and service from a particular store.

---

cus|tom|er da|ta /kʌstəmər deɪtə/

MARKETING

NOUN **Customer data** is information held on file about customers by a store or other business, usually including names, contact details, and buying habits.

○ *Customer data are the firsthand responses that are obtained from customers through investigation or by asking direct questions.*

○ *The loyalty card helps the company gather customer data, such as individual preferences and spending patterns.*

---

cus|tom|er ex|pe|ri|ence /kʌstəmər ɪkspɪəriəns/

MARKETING

NOUN **Customer experience** is what customers feel while shopping, affected by such factors as how a store is laid out, the level of service they receive, and how easy it is to find products.

○ *To provide an improved customer experience, the entire company was involved in a series of service-driven initiatives.*

○ *The company, which is dedicated to customer service, has undertaken wide-ranging research to enhance customer experience.*

cus|tom|er-fac|ing /kʌstəmər feɪsɪŋ/

SERVICE

ADJECTIVE **Customer-facing** activities are those in which you are interacting or communicating directly with your customers.

○ *Customer-facing staff play a pivotal role in the experiences consumers have, and through social interaction communicate powerful messages directly to the consumer.*

○ *The attitude of customer-facing staff can make a big difference to the shopping experience and can really influence sales.*

cus|tom|er flow /kʌstəmər floʊ/ (**customer flows**)

MARKETING

NOUN **Customer flow** is the movement of customers around a store.

○ *Providing more check-outs increased customer flow, reduced bottlenecks and improved sales.*

○ *By siting the restaurant on the top floor, the store management has directed customer flow through other departments.*

cus|tom|er pref|er|ence /kʌstəmər prɛfərəns/ (**customer preferences**)

MARKETING

NOUN **Customer preference** is what type of product an individual customer likes and dislikes.

○ *The sweetener blend added to the company's most famous brand is formulated for each country based on customer preference.*

○ *Our club card used at physical outlets and the order records from our online presence means we can readily establish individual customer preference.*

cus|tom|er pro|file /kʌstəmər proʊfaɪl/ (**customer profiles**)

MARKETING

NOUN **Customer profiles** are records held about individual customers, used as a guide for determining whom to target with certain products, and including details such as age, gender, and spending patterns.

○ *Up-to-date and accurate customer profile information is vital to successful marketing.*

○ *Asking customers to fill in questionnaires and do reviews are good ways to build up customer profiles and thus target new products.*

---

cus|tom|er ser|vice /kʌstəmər sɜrvɪs/

SERVICE

NOUN **Customer service** is any activity designed to increase the level of customer satisfaction, such as help with finding the right product and guidance about its use.

○ *A person who has experienced poor customer service will most likely share their bad experience with an average of ten other people and cost your business money.*

○ *Retailers can keep the customers coming back with customer-friendly policies and by training employees to provide excellent customer service.*

---

cus|tom|er sup|port /kʌstəmər səpɔrt/

SERVICE

NOUN **Customer support** is a service provided to help customers resolve any technical problems that they may have with a product or service.

○ *When people have problems or want to ask a question about a product, they contact customer support.*

○ *Staff at our customer support centers coordinate returns and repairs as well as offering customers guidance on trouble-shooting.*

---

cus|tom-made /kʌstəm meɪd/

PRODUCTS

ADJECTIVE When something is **custom-made**, it is made to the customer's specifications.

○ *Generally speaking, a custom-made garment will cost more than an off-the-rack garment.*

○ *Our suits are custom-made and the client may require several fittings.*

cut-price /kʌt praɪs/

PRICING

ADJECTIVE **Cut-price** goods are available at prices or rates below the standard price or rate.

○ *Thrift shops are sought out by students for their cut-price fashions.*

○ *With off-peak deals and cut-price tickets, more people than ever can afford to travel abroad.*

C|V|C /si vi si/ (short for **card validation code**)

PAYMENT TECHNOLOGY

ABBREVIATION The **CVC** is an added security feature on credit cards, in the form of an extra 3 or 4 numbers printed on the back of the card.

○ *As a security measure, e-retailers often request the CVC code printed on the back of the credit card.*

○ *CVCs are one way to make sure someone paying by phone or on the Internet has the actual credit card in his or her possession.*

Dd

de|liv|er /dɪlɪvər/ (delivers, delivered, delivering)

DISTRIBUTION

TRANSITIVE/INTRANSITIVE VERB To **deliver** goods and services is to carry or convey them from the seller to the buyer.

○ When the goods are delivered, the owner should check the number of cartons unloaded against the carrier's delivery receipt so that none are overlooked.

○ We will deliver your order between noon and 1p.m.

de|liv|er|y /dɪlɪvəri/

DISTRIBUTION

NOUN **Delivery** is the sending out and receiving of goods or services at an arranged place.

○ The florist provides a delivery service to bring flowers and gifts to local hospitals.

○ Does your local supermarket offer a delivery service?

de|part|ment /dɪpɑrtmənt/ (departments)

STORE FIXTURES AND LAYOUT

NOUN If a store is divided into **departments**, it has separate areas within it where goods of different categories are displayed and sold.

○ These stores are characterized by wide product mixes and organized into separate departments to facilitate marketing efforts and internal management.

○ Good clear signage is needed to direct customers to a store's various departments.

de|part|ment store /dɪpɑ̱rtmənt stɔr/ (**department stores**)

OUTLETS

NOUN A **department store** is a large store, divided into departments which sell such products as furnishings, electronics, clothing, footwear, toys, cosmetics, and sometimes also groceries.

○ *The central message of department store merchandising is that customers can find just about anything they want in the store and under one roof.*

○ *A department store has several departments housed under the same roof to facilitate buying, customer service, and merchandising.*

de|sign|er cloth|ing /dɪza̱ɪnər klo̱ʊðɪŋ/

PRODUCTS

NOUN **Designer clothing** is fashionable or luxury clothing made by, or carrying the label of, a well-known fashion designer.

○ *The store's designer clothing range, featuring big name brands, has sold well.*

○ *The department store specializes in designer clothing from leading fashion houses.*

des|ti|na|tion store /de̱stɪneɪʃ°n stɔr/ (**destination stores**)

OUTLETS

NOUN A **destination store** draws customers by selling unusual items, or having a friendly atmosphere, special pricing, and other desirable characteristics.

○ *The company designs its stores to be destination stores, generating their own traffic, but in the general vicinity of major retail shopping.*

○ *It's not enough for a destination store just to attract customers from a long distance away but those customers have to be persuaded to spend money there.*

▶ SYNONYM:
anchor store

de|stock /dɪstɒ̱k/ (**destocks, destocked, destocking**)

MERCHANDISING

TRANSITIVE/INTRANSITIVE VERB To **destock** is to reduce the amount of stock held or to stop holding stock of certain products.

○ *Active destocking refers to an active decision to reduce the inventory to sales ratio of a company.*

○ *Retailers reduced their inventories as consumers tightened their belts and the manufacturing sector responded by destocking; in other words, they have reduced their output.*

---

dis|count¹ /dɪskaʊnt/ (discounts)

PRICING

NOUN When goods are offered at a **discount** their usual selling price is reduced.

○ *A firm may receive quantity discounts if its orders are large enough.*

○ *The greater the discount, the larger the volume of stock that is moved.*

Adjectives used with "discount"

○ *The sale offers **deep** discounts on ski and snowboard apparel and gear.*

○ *The chain gives employees a **generous** discount to encourage them to wear its brand.*

○ *Both stores are selling electrical goods at a **hefty** discount during the sale.*

○ *Many Internet retailers are offering **steep** discounts and free shipping.*

○ *The voucher entitles you to a **substantial** discount on all products bought online.*

---

dis|count² /dɪskaʊnt/ (discounts, discounted, discounting)

PRICING

VERB If a store **discounts** goods, it reduces the usual price of the goods, often by a stated percentage or amount.

○ *In many cases, you just won't be able to tell if an item in that store is at full retail price or discounted.*

○ *Dead stock is sent to a specialist off-price retailer where it is heavily discounted.*

---

dis|count store /dɪskaʊnt stɔr/ (discount stores)

OUTLETS

NOUN A **discount store** is one in which goods are sold at low prices.

○ *The major discount stores are offering the machine for $44, a discount of 12% on the RRP of $50.*

○ *Leading midmarket supermarkets continue to see market share drop with customers favoring discount stores and upmarket specialist stores.*

---

dis|play¹ /dɪspleɪ/ (displays)

MERCHANDISING

NOUN A **display** is an arrangement of goods laid out to show them off at their best and so that customers can see what is on offer.

○ *Cast your vote for your favorite artistic display in the retail windows in the mall.*

○ *The displays of goods in the store all had an Easter theme.*

---

dis|play² /dɪspleɪ/ (displays, displayed, displaying)

MERCHANDISING

VERB To **display** goods is to lay them out to show them off.

○ *In response to customer desires, we are changing the way we decide which products to display on endcaps.*

○ *Bridal gowns should be displayed to maximum advantage and not crammed onto rails.*

---

dis|play case /dɪspleɪ keɪs/ (display cases)

STORE FIXTURES AND LAYOUT

NOUN A **display case** is an enclosed structure for showing goods, often high-value goods such as jewellery.

○ *This glass display case in silver with lockable glass doors is for displaying trophies, jewelry, china, ornaments, and other retail or exhibition products.*

○ *In the retail fittings section of the show, various companies are exhibiting the latest range of refrigerated display cases and cabinets.*

---

dis|tri|bu|tion /dɪstrɪbyuʃ°n/

DISTRIBUTION

NOUN A business, or part of a business, involved in **distribution** is concerned with moving goods to where they are needed.

○ *The regional distribution centers are usually located away from urban areas, but always near a major road to facilitate transporting the merchandise to the individual stores.*

○ *The order is completed by the manager, transmitted to the relevant distribution center, and picked up from dispatch the next day.*

---

dis|trib|u|tor /dɪstrɪbyətər/ (distributors)

`PERSONNEL`

NOUN A **distributor** is a business involved in moving goods to where they are needed, often from a central point on a road or rail network to the surrounding area.

○ *Food distributors sell their inventory to grocery stores.*

○ *The online digital entertainment business was previously owned by a US distributor and wholesaler of home entertainment products.*

---

drop-ship /drɒp ʃɪp/ (drop-ships, drop-shipped, drop-shipping)

`DISTRIBUTION`

VERB To **drop-ship** an item is to have it sent direct from your supplier to your customer. This is a common method of fulfilling online orders.

○ *One of the most popular ways to sell wholesale products at a profit is to drop-ship them.*

○ *When the goods are drop-shipped, no inventory is held and the retailer is not involved in the shipping.*

---

drop ship|ment /drɒp ʃɪpmənt/ (drop shipments)

`DISTRIBUTION`

NOUN A **drop shipment** is a delivery sent direct to a customer from a supplier without first being delivered to the retailer with whom the order was placed and to whom payment was made.

○ *Drop shipments are delivered to the store by the manufacturer and billed to the retailer through a wholesaler or the headquarters of a chain.*

○ *The most common way of fulfilling orders taken by Internet-based retailers is via drop shipment.*

dun /dʌn/ (duns, dunned, dunning)

SUPPLIER ACCOUNTS

VERB If someone **duns** you **for** money you owe them, they ask you again and again for payment.

○ *The computer helps generate letters dunning customers for payment.*

○ *You dun your customers when you remind them that overdue items still need to be paid.*

du|ty /duti/

SUPPLIER ACCOUNTS

NOUN **Duty** is a government tax added to the cost of a certain category of goods, such as alcohol, tobacco, or imports and exports.

○ *Most countries charge customs duties and tax on items shipped from the U. S.*

○ *Customs duty is a tax on the importation and exportation of goods.*

du|ty-free /duti fri/

SUPPLIER ACCOUNTS

ADJECTIVE **Duty-free** goods are exempt from the government tax normally charged on that category of goods.

○ *A special limited edition of this single malt whisky will be available at the Mumbai and Delhi duty-free shops from October.*

○ *Duty-free retail sales at their airport stores, especially of liquor and tobacco products, have grown significantly.*

d

Ee

e-com|merce /i kɒmərs/

GENERAL

NOUN **E-commerce** is the buying, selling, and ordering of goods and services using the Internet.

○ *Retailers are aware of the potential profitability of e-commerce or online shopping.*

○ *As the collective wisdom of the online crowd displaces traditional advertising, the roaring engines of e-commerce are being stoked by favorable reviews.*

> **WORD BUILDER**
> **e-** = using the Internet
>
> The prefix **e-** appears in nouns that refer to an activity or process done using the Internet: **e-commerce**, **e-payment**, **e-tail**.

E|D|I /i di aɪ/ (short for **electronic data interchange**)

PAYMENT TECHNOLOGY

ABBREVIATION **EDI** is an electronic system that allows a supplier and a retailer to communicate easily.

○ *Electronic orders placed through EDI or the Internet are processed with little or no human involvement or time delays.*

○ *A company has persuaded all its suppliers to move over to transmission of invoices via EDI, which allows processing without any data rekeying.*

E|F|T /i ɛf ti/ (short for **electronic funds transfer**)

PAYMENT TECHNOLOGY

ABBREVIATION **EFT** is a transfer of funds that is carried out by electronic means, such as a computer.

○ *EFT systems eliminate the paperwork of purchase orders, invoices, and checks.*

○ *The monthly installment will be electronically deducted from her account by EFT.*

EFT|POS /ɛftpɒs/ (short for **electronic funds transfer point of sale**)

PAYMENT TECHNOLOGY

ABBREVIATION **EFTPOS** is a system for deducting the cost of a purchase direct from the customer's bank, building-society, or credit-card account by means of a computer link using the telephone network.

○ *I'd already paid by EFTPOS and didn't have 10c for the plastic bag so had to break a $20 bill.*

○ *With EFTPOS the money is wired directly into the retailer's account, and the shopper does not need cash on hand, credit cards, or a check book to make a purchase.*

---

e|lec|tron|ic re|ceipt /ɪlɛktrɒnɪk rɪsiːt/ (**electronic receipts**)

PAYMENT TECHNOLOGY

NOUN An **electronic receipt** is one created in a computerized cash register, or by an online retailer. It will usually show the date and time, how payment is made, and other details of the sale.

○ *Many companies now offer electronic receipts, either e-mailed or uploaded to password-protected websites.*

○ *Electronic receipts mean that you no longer have to worry about losing all those paper receipts that clutter your wallet or pocketbook.*

---

e|lec|tron|ics /ɪlɛktrɒnɪks/

PRODUCTS

NOUN **Electronics** is the product category name for consumer goods that are powered by the flow of electrons, for example computers, point-and-shoot cameras, and cellphones.

○ *Laptops have been the bestselling products in the electronics category.*

○ *Sales of larger items in the electronics category, such as gaming machines and TVs, have been disappointing.*

E

em|ploy|ee dis|count /ɪmplɔ̯i dɪskaʊnt/ (**employee discounts**)

CUSTOMER ACCOUNTS

NOUN When the employees of a store or other retail business are entitled to an **employee discount**, they do not have to pay the full price for goods they buy in the store.

- ○ Even with the employee discount of my buddy who works at the store, it still cost me over $100.

- ○ When creating store policy, decide what percentage of employee discount and sales commission you will offer the staff.

em|po|ri|um /ɛmpɔ̯riəm/ (**emporiums**)

OUTLETS

NOUN An **emporium** is a large store or shop selling a wide variety of merchandise.

- ○ When first introduced, the emporium was actually a department store with a wide variety of things for sale.

- ○ Their award-winning store is described as an emporium of delights, a new concept in retail with its own concierge and themed fitting rooms.

en|cryp|tion /ɪnkrɪpʃᵊn/

PAYMENT TECHNOLOGY

NOUN **Encryption** is any system for security and fraud prevention which automatically breaks up and reorders information before it is sent via telephone lines or the Internet.

- ○ It is a system that relies on heavy encryption and state-of-the-art security.

- ○ Encryption is the conversion of data into a form that cannot be easily understood by an unauthorized person, and is important to make electronic transactions secure.

end cap /ɛnd kæp/ (**end caps**)

STORE FIXTURES AND LAYOUT

NOUN An **end cap** is a rack or counter at the end of a store aisle used to display promotional or sale items.

○ *Frequent rotation of products displayed on end caps rather than the regular shelves often makes economic sense because they grab customers' attention.*

○ *Products displayed on end caps nearest to the checkout counters are often picked up by customers as they wait to pay.*

---

end|ing in|ven|to|ry /ɛndɪŋ ɪnvᵊntɔri/ (**ending inventories**)

MERCHANDISING

NOUN **Ending inventory** is the amount or value of stock at the end of a specified period.

○ *An item's inventory change equals its ending inventory value minus its beginning inventory value.*

○ *If your actual ending inventory (i.e. beginning inventory less the value of sales and markdowns), is within five percent of what you had planned, you are doing well.*

---

e-pay|ment /ipeɪmənt/ (**e-payments**)

PAYMENT TECHNOLOGY

NOUN **E-payments** are electronic payments for transactions made on the Internet.

○ *More and more people are turning to electronic payment – or e-payment – as an alternative to sending checks through the mail.*

○ *E-payments can be made direct using a credit or debit card or via a secure global acquirer such as PayPal.*

E|POS /ipɒs/ (short for **electronic point of sale**)

PAYMENT TECHNOLOGY

ABBREVIATION **EPOS** is any computerized system, which may include devices such as barcode readers, scanners, and touchscreens, used to record sales and control stock.

○ *Our reliable touchscreen EPOS is easy to use and enables fast transactions.*

○ *Because EPOS systems automatically identify items purchased, the time to pass through a checkout counter is reduced.*

e-tail /ˈiteɪl/

OUTLETS

NOUN **E-tail** is retail carried out via the Internet.

○ *Many e-tail stores have online forums and ratings that allow customers to express their views and opinions.*

○ *Many e-tail stores have online forums that allow customers to express their opinions on a given product, a community aspect that bricks-and-mortar retail stores can never hope to provide.*

ex|port¹ /ˈɛkspɔrt/ (exports)

DISTRIBUTION

NOUN **Exports** are goods or services sent out from one country for sale in another country.

○ *These items are highly demanded by our customers and are popular in the national as well as in the international export market.*

○ *Although they do supply local retailers, most of the manufacturer's turnover comes from exports, especially to the European market.*

ex|port² /ɪkˈspɔrt/ (exports, exported, exporting)

DISTRIBUTION

VERB Companies **export** their goods or services when they send them out of their own country to be sold in another country, or countries.

○ *Almost half of its products are exported, with the remainder sold in the home market.*

○ *Most Scotch whisky is exported making it an important contributor to the economy.*

Ff

fac|to|ry out|let /fǽktəri aʊtlɪt/ (factory outlets)

OUTLETS

NOUN A **factory outlet** is a premises in which a manufacturer offers goods for sale direct to the public. Such outlets are often cheaper than retail stores because retail costs are not included.

○ Factory outlets are owned and operated by manufacturers and normally carry the manufacturers' surplus, discontinued, or irregular goods.

○ The knitwear company has a factory outlet in addition to selling to high-end clothing retailers around the world.

fas|ci|a /féɪʃə/ (fascias)

MARKETING

NOUN The **fascia** on a shop or store front is any surface on the outside of the shop or store that displays the company name, company logo, and company color scheme.

○ The fascia is the most visible part of a retail brand – it is the name of the retailer, but it is also the logo and the graphics.

○ The store has had a complete makeover, including a new fascia sporting the new logo.

FI|FO /fáɪfoʊ/ (short for **first in, first out**)

MANAGEMENT ACCOUNTS

ABBREVIATION **FIFO** is a method of accounting which assumes that the oldest stock is sold first.

○ FIFO is normally the method used for stock rotation, where the oldest stock is used/sold in preference to newer stock.

○ The FIFO method assumes that goods are withdrawn from stock in the order in which they are received.

> **RELATED WORDS**
>
> Compare **FIFO** with **LIFO** which is a method of valuing inventory which assumes that the newest stock is sold first.

F

fire sale /faɪər seɪl/ (fire sales)

MERCHANDISING

NOUN A **fire sale** is a sale of goods at reduced prices, either after a fire at a store or factory or simply to raise money in an emergency.

○ In the retail trade a "fire sale" typically takes place after a fire, to get rid of fire-damaged merchandise.

○ The store was careful never to mention the phrase "fire sale" when clearing stock after a recent fire in one of its branches.

firsts /fɜrsts/

PRODUCTS

NOUN **Firsts** are saleable goods of the highest quality.

○ It is important to know if items are firsts or seconds as often the appearance of the piece will give no indication of it being substandard.

○ Quality control determines if the factory products are firsts, which can command the highest price and the widest market, or seconds.

fit|ting room (in Brit use **changing room**) /fɪtɪŋ rum/ (fitting rooms)

STORE FIXTURES AND LAYOUT

NOUN The **fitting rooms** in a store are cubicles for customers to use when trying on clothes, usually having mirrors and separate female and male sections.

○ The designer created state-of-the-art fitting rooms at fashion stores in New York, with music and adjustable lighting.

○ Keep the fitting rooms clean and tidy and free of discarded hangers, tags, and empty packaging.

fix|ture /fɪkstʃər/ (fixtures)

NOUN The **fixtures** in a store or shop are the shelves or shelving units that products are displayed on.

○ *Retail fixtures and displays include gridwall, slatwall, display cases, retail shelving, greeting card racks, clothing racks, mannequins, and hangers.*

○ *Refurbishment of the store included getting rid of old fixtures and bringing in sleek modern ones.*

f

TYPES OF FIXTURE

The following are all types of fixture that are found in stores:

corner rack
a shelving unit designed to fit into corners to maximize space

cube unit
a shelving unit made up of horizontal and vertical dividers which form open-ended cubes, suitable for displaying products such as towels in a range of colors

display case
an enclosed structure for showing goods, often high-value goods such as jewelry

end cap
a rack or counter at the end of a store aisle used to display promotional or sale items

garment rack
a rail used in stores to hang items of clothing on display, such as shirts and coats

gridwall panel
a metal grid that can be hung on a wall and used for displaying goods

slatwall panel
a slatted surface that can be fixed to the wall from which shelves or hooks can be hung at varying heights to display merchandise

F

flag|ship store /flægʃɪp stɔr/ (flagship stores)

OUTLETS

NOUN A **flagship store** is the most important store in a chain, often with the largest volume of sales, or the most up-to-date formats or layouts.

○ It is usual that the opening of a flagship store marks the first development of a retail store portfolio within a luxury fashion retailer's most important foreign markets.

○ The European chain's new US flagship store is the latest anchor for the shopping mall, following the opening of a cinema and food court.

flash sale /flæʃ seɪl/ (flash sales)

MERCHANDISING

NOUN A **flash sale** is a sale, held for a very limited time, offering very large discounts on surplus stock.

○ With an air of exclusivity and luxury brand names, flash sale websites host limited-time sales for members only.

○ Flash sales are a proven and successful method of selling for suppliers seeking to liquidate unsold capacity or off-season stocks.

float /floʊt/ (floats)

CUSTOMER ACCOUNTS

NOUN The **float** is a sum of money in a cash register used to provide change at the start of the day's business.

○ Smaller stores can benefit from the system, as it frees up a lot of the manager's time that used to be taken up with organizing till floats, and counting cash after each shift.

○ The till drawer and its float is checked by a supervisor after each shift.

floor|walk|er (in BRIT use **shopwalker**) /flɔrwɔkər/ (floorwalkers)

PERSONNEL

NOUN A **floorwalker** is a person who supervises salespersons in a store and advises customers.

○ *The floorwalkers should be readily identifiable, possibly wearing a brightly colored jacket or T-shirt.*

○ *The floorwalker is supposed to be able to tell the prospective customer at what counter any article may be purchased, and just how to find that counter.*

F|M|C|G /ɛf ɛm si dʒi/ (short for **fast-moving consumer goods**)
PRODUCTS

ABBREVIATION **FMCG** are retail items that are bought frequently, such as coffee, tea, milk, and bread.

○ *FMCG goods are the quickest items to leave the shelves at a supermarket, and usually have the lowest price due to that fact.*

○ *FMCG retailers specialize in products with a relatively short shelf life, either because they have a high turnover or because the products deteriorate quickly.*

F|O|B /ɛf oʊ bi/ (short for **freight on board**)
DISTRIBUTION

ABBREVIATION **FOB** is a shipping term used to indicate whether it is the seller or buyer who is responsible for paying for shipping or carrier costs, and when ownership of the goods transfers from one to the other.

○ *Selling goods on an FOB basis enables the seller to get paid more quickly as their responsibility ends once cargo is loaded onto ship or aircraft.*

○ *FOB indicates that the seller provides transportation from the factory to trucks or railcars, after which the buyer pays all the carrier charges.*

---

food court /fud kɔrt/ (**food courts**)
OUTLETS

NOUN A **food court** is an area, usually in a shopping mall, airport or railway station, where several catering outlets are grouped together with shared seating.

○ *The most common type of food court is an area in a shopping mall where fast food is sold around a common eating area.*

○ *A stop-off at the mall food court is a favorite for families looking for a quick meal.*

foot|wear /fʊtwɛər/

PRODUCTS

NOUN **Footwear** is the retail product category that includes shoes and boots.

○ *In the footwear category, sales of fur-lined boots have soared after the heavy snow last winter.*

○ *New stock of summer footwear including sandals and espadrilles has just arrived.*

> **WORD BUILDER**
> **-wear** = clothing that is intended for a particular type of person or a particular area of the body: **babywear**, **childrenswear**, **footwear**

for|ward|ing a|gent /fɔrwərdɪŋ eɪdʒənt/ (**forwarding agents**)

DISTRIBUTION

NOUN A **forwarding agent** is a person, agency, or business involved in the collection, shipment, and delivery of goods.

○ *A forwarding agent is a person or company that organizes shipments for individuals or other companies.*

○ *Exporters often use independent forwarding agents who offer a full range of freight forwarding services by air, sea, overland, or courier.*

fran|chise /fræntʃaɪz/ (**franchises**)

OUTLETS

NOUN A **franchise** is a type of retail business in which an individual or group is granted the right to market a company's goods or services within a certain territory or location.

○ *Many fast-food companies operate franchises.*

○ *The major alternative to the continued expansion of the retail chain is the franchise concept in which an individual entrepreneur operates a business in conjunction with a network of suppliers.*

fre|quent shop|per pro|gram (BRIT **frequent shopper programme**) /frikwənt ʃɒpər proʊgræm/ (**frequent shopper programs**)

MARKETING

NOUN A **frequent shopper program** is one that rewards customers for purchases made on multiple visits, and builds up points entitling them to reduced prices and free items.

  ○ Frequent shopper programs are becoming ubiquitous in retailing, although retailers seem unsure if they are leading to higher loyalty, or to higher profits.

  ○ Nearly two-thirds of all US households believe it is important to shop in stores that offer a frequent shopper program or loyalty card program.

front|age /frʌntɪdʒ/

MARKETING

NOUN A store's **frontage** is its outside walls and windows that can be seen from the street or as you approach the entrance.

  ○ Most retailers want lots of street frontage to showcase their wares, while second floor space usually goes to offices.

  ○ He chose the location because he knew the Main Street frontage would attract customers.

ful|fill|ment (or **fulfilment**) /fʊlfɪlmənt/

DISTRIBUTION

NOUN **Fulfillment** is the process or a way of managing customer orders from source to delivery.

  ○ Fulfillment services include taking orders from our clients, managing and locating their stock, picking and packing accurately, and getting the order to their customer on time.

  ○ Every major retailer requires its suppliers to meet stringent fulfillment requirements including on-time delivery and order accuracy.

Gg

gar|ment rack /gɑrmənt ræk/ (garment racks)

STORE FIXTURES AND LAYOUT

NOUN A **garment rack** is a rail used in stores to hang items of clothing on display, such as shirts and coats.

- ○ *Folding garment racks are easy to transport or store, making them popular for many retail uses in clothing stores.*
- ○ *We supply sturdy chrome garment racks designed to withstand tough retail environments.*

▶ **SYNONYM:**
clothes rail

gen|er|al ledg|er /dʒɛnrəl lɛdʒər/ (general ledgers)

MANAGEMENT ACCOUNTS

NOUN The **general ledger** is a part of a business's financial records and includes the balance sheet, profit and loss, and expense account.

- ○ *The general ledger is the accounting transaction record, maintained either manually or using computer software, of all the balance sheet and income statement balances of a company or business.*
- ○ *The five main types of general ledger accounts are asset account, liability account, expense account, revenue account, and equity account.*

gift card /gɪft kɑrd/ (gift cards)

SERVICE

NOUN If someone buys you a **gift card** from a store, they buy a card of a certain value that allows you to choose an item or items of that value at that store or chain.

- ○ *Gift cards from bookstores make great last-minute Christmas and holiday gifts when you are unsure what to buy.*

○ *The music chain's gift cards will be stocked and sold by a number of other major retailers, with the aim of attracting more customers to their remaining stores.*

---

gift cer|tif|i|cate /gɪft sərtɪfɪkɪt/ (**gift certificates**)

SERVICE

NOUN A **gift certificate** is a voucher for goods or services bought by one customer and given to and spent by another.

○ *We've developed several gift certificate choices for anniversary, birthday, and Christmas.*

○ *The law provides that gift cards and gift certificates cannot expire within five years from the date they were activated.*

---

gift re|ceipt /gɪft rɪsit/ (**gift receipts**)

SERVICE

NOUN A **gift receipt** shows proof of purchase but leaves out the amount spent. It can be used to return goods given as a gift.

○ *If you have bought someone a present, you can give them the gift receipt in case they don't like it, and then they can take it back to the store and exchange it for something else.*

○ *The price isn't shown on the gift receipt.*

---

gift|wrap /gɪftræp/

SERVICE

NOUN **Giftwrap** is decorative paper for occasions such as birthdays or anniversaries.

○ *Sales of giftwrap are growing by only 5 to 8 percent a year with the typical price about $2 a roll.*

○ *The store sells giftwrap for every occasion: birthdays, anniversaries, Christmas, and weddings.*

---

gift-wrap /gɪft ræp/ (**gift-wraps, gift-wrapped, gift-wrapping**)

SERVICE

VERB If you ask a store to **gift-wrap** your purchase, you ask them to wrap it in special paper.

○ *Online stores often have a box to check if you want your purchase gift-wrapped.*

○ *Since the sweater is for my husband's birthday, would you gift-wrap it?*

---

gon|do|la /gɒndᵊlə/ (gondolas)

STORE FIXTURES AND LAYOUT

NOUN A **gondola** is a shelving unit used to form rows and aisles in stores. A gondola can be adapted to display goods on both sides, or at either end of the row.

○ *The gondola is usually designed to be at eye-level height and will consist of a central panel, which sits on a rectangular frame with castors underneath.*

○ *Most supermarket aisles are made up of gondola units.*

---

goods /gʊdz/

PRODUCTS

NOUN **Goods** are things that are made to be sold.

○ *Money can be exchanged for goods or services.*

○ *Britain's main trading partners have been trapped in low or no growth, unable to buy more goods and services.*

---

gra|tis /grætɪs/

SERVICE

ADVERB When something is offered **gratis**, it is free of charge.

○ *Some services must be paid for but alterations to garments can be made gratis.*

○ *Catalogues are mailed gratis to all club members.*

---

grid mer|chan|dis|er /grɪd mɜrtʃəndaɪzər/ (grid merchandisers)

STORE FIXTURES AND LAYOUT

NOUN A **grid merchandiser** is a lightweight, free-standing, flexible fixture made up of moveable grids of wire and used by retailers to display large volumes of merchandise in a small space.

○ *A grid merchandiser is a simple and inexpensive way to add display capacity.*

○ *This grid merchandiser, made of powder-coated steel, is suitable for supermarket or smaller retail store displays.*

grid|wall pan|el /grɪdwɔl pænᵊl/ (gridwall panels)

STORE FIXTURES AND LAYOUT

NOUN A **gridwall panel** is a metal grid that can be hung on a wall and used for displaying goods.

○ *Gridwall panels can be freestanding or mounted on the wall and can hold shelves, hooks, bins, or other hanging attachments.*

○ *Gridwall panels make for flexible and adaptable displays, especially where an assortment of products, such as sports apparel and equipment, is to be displayed.*

gro|cer /groʊsər/ (grocers)

OUTLETS

NOUN A **grocer** is an individual, company, or chain selling foodstuffs.

○ *This report ranks the top grocers based on free-range and eco-friendly products.*

○ *Asian food grocers are good places to find more exotic ingredients not available in your local supermarket.*

gross[1] /groʊs/

MANAGEMENT ACCOUNTS

ADJECTIVE **Gross** refers to the total amount of something, especially money, before anything has been taken away.

○ *This is a fixed-rate account guaranteeing 10.4 percent gross interest or 7.8 percent net.*

○ *Annual gross revenue from the new store is expected to be about $5 million.*

▶ **COLLOCATIONS:**
gross amount
gross revenue
gross sales
gross total

RELATED WORDS

Compare **gross** with **net** which refers to the amount of something that remains after subtracting taxes, expenses, losses, and costs.

gross² /grəʊs/ (grosses, grossed, grossing)

MANAGEMENT ACCOUNTS

VERB If a person or a company **grosses** a particular amount of money, they earn it as total revenue, before deductions such as expenses and tax.

○ *The popular brand grossed $65 million in sales last year.*

○ *By her third year, she was grossing $6 million, thanks to a fortuitous contract with the superstore.*

gross prof|it /grəʊs prɒfɪt/ (gross profits)

MANAGEMENT ACCOUNTS

NOUN A company's **gross profit** is the difference between its total income from sales and its total production costs. Also known informally as "the gross."

○ *Gross profit is the figure obtained on the profit and loss account when the cost of goods sold is deducted from the sales revenue of a business.*

○ *A typical luxury car makes a gross profit of around 15–20 percent of its sales price, and small cars barely break even.*

▶ SYNONYM:
gross margin

gross prof|it mar|gin /grəʊs prɒfɪt mɑrdʒɪn/ (gross profit margins)

MANAGEMENT ACCOUNTS

NOUN A **gross profit margin** is a measure of the profitability of a company, that is calculated by dividing gross profit by net sales.

○ *Trade publications claim that the chain's gross profit margins approach 10 percent, well above the industry norm.*

○ *A reasonable approximation of cost must be given, usually by deducting a gross profit margin from the full selling price.*

▶ SYNONYMS:
gross margin percentage
gross profit percentage
gross margin ratio

guar|an|tee /gǽrənti/ (**guarantees**)

SERVICE

NOUN A **guarantee** is a written promise that a manufacturer or retailer will repair a product or give you a new one, if the product has a fault.

○ *They offer a 30-day money back guarantee on most of their products.*

○ *Most large household appliances come with a year's guarantee.*

> **Talking about guarantees**
>
> If a product is **under** guarantee, it is protected by a guarantee at that particular time.
>
> If a product is **covered** by a guarantee, it is protected by it.
>
> If a guarantee **covers** or **includes** a particular thing, that thing is written in the guarantee.

g

hab|er|dash|er|y /hæbərdæʃəri/

PRODUCTS

NOUN **Haberdashery** is men's clothing and accessories.

○ He bought a new tie and gloves at the haberdashery counter.

○ The rate of tax on handkerchiefs and scarves is reduced to 5 percent and the 25 percent rate on other articles of haberdashery is increased to 30 percent.

hang|er /hæŋər/ (hangers)

STORE FIXTURES AND LAYOUT

NOUN A **hanger** is a rigid metal, plastic, or wooden device on which a single piece of clothing, such as a coat or dress, is hung.

○ Padded hangers are used to prevent creases in luxury fabric items.

○ The higher cost and thickness of wood makes it impractical to choose wooden hangers for displaying tee shirts.

hang tag /hæŋ tæg/ (hang tags)

STORE FIXTURES AND LAYOUT

NOUN A **hang tag** is a small cardboard or plastic label that hangs from an item of clothing and gives information such as size, color, fabric, and price.

○ Hang tags can play a valuable role in attracting consumer attention and relaying important information about the product to which the tags are attached.

○ Labels may be affixed to the product in the form of a hang tag using string or similar material.

hard|ware /hɑrdwɛər/

PRODUCTS

NOUN **Hardware** is the product category name for items of ironmongery such as locks, nuts, bolts, and nails.

○ A growth in the popularity of home improvement has been reflected in increased sales from hardware retail outlets.

○ The hardware store stocks hand tools, and every type of nut, bolt, and nail you can think of.

home de|liv|er|y /hoʊm dɪlɪvəri/

DISTRIBUTION

NOUN **Home delivery** is the bringing of items to the customer's home rather than the customer taking or collecting them from the store.

○ In the first cash-and-carry stores, items were sold only for cash; no credit was extended, and no expensive home deliveries were provided.

○ For customers who want to avoid paying for home delivery, click and collect is becoming a popular option.

home en|ter|tain|ment /hoʊm ɛntərteɪnmənt/

PRODUCTS

NOUN **Home entertainment** is the product category name for electrical goods that include TVs, sound systems, DVD players, and games consoles.

○ The company is a supplier and installer of audiovisual home entertainment products, offering a complete range of audiovisual and home automation equipment and systems.

○ Electronics and home entertainment, especially plasma TVs, were the standout product categories.

house|hold goods /haʊshoʊld gʊdz/

PRODUCTS

NOUN **Household goods** is the product category name for goods used in and around the home, such as cleaning products.

○ Department stores began with the mass retailing of apparel and textiles and then of furniture and other household goods.

○ *The category buyer keeps up to date with wholesale trade suppliers and manufacturers of housewares and household goods.*

> The following are all categories of products found in department stores.
>
> apparel, accessories, babywear, childrenswear, electronics, footwear, haberdashery, homewares, home entertainment, interiors, lighting, nursery, soft furnishings

H

house|wares /ha͟ʊswɛərz/
PRODUCTS

NOUN **Housewares** is the product category name for equipment used in the home, such as pots and pans and dishes.

○ *The home furnishings division includes decorative home products, bedding and bath, housewares for the kitchen, luggage, rugs, picture frames, crystal, silver, and framed art.*

○ *Pots and pans and other housewares are on the first floor.*

hy|per|mar|ket /ha͟ɪpərmɑrkɪt/ (hypermarkets)
OUTLETS

NOUN A **hypermarket** is a huge self-service store, usually on the outskirts of a town.

○ *Are consumers increasingly choosing hypermarkets for their convenient, one-stop-shop offering?*

○ *Smaller stores are likely to suffer as the huge hypermarkets become more convenient than convenience stores for consumers with a long shopping list and plenty of time to drive out-of-town.*

im|port¹ /ˈɪmpɔrt/ (imports)

DISTRIBUTION

NOUN **Imports** are goods brought into the country from another country.

○ *Cheap imports have destroyed the home-grown apparel manufacturing sector.*

○ *Imports of fruit and vegetables from the other side of the world often have a large carbon footprint.*

im|port² /ɪmˈpɔrt/ (imports, imported, importing)

DISTRIBUTION

VERB To **import** is to bring goods in from another country.

○ *Large-volume discount stores that sell the most inexpensive products import from low-cost suppliers in the Far East.*

○ *Cotton and other raw materials imported from around the world have risen in price.*

in|de|pend|ent /ɪndɪˈpɛndənt/

OUTLETS

ADJECTIVE An **independent** retailer is one that is not part of the big retail chains.

○ *The independent retailer cannot compete with the large-scale retailer in economies of buying.*

○ *An independent retailer is one who builds his or his business from the ground up.*

in|stall|ment (BRIT **instalment**) /ɪnstɔ́lmənt/ (**installments**)

NOUN An **installment** is one of the amounts, usually equal, into which a debt is divided for payment at stated intervals over a fixed period.

○ *The purchase price is payable by the client in six equal installments.*

○ *If you have a good credit rating, we may be able to arrange payment by installments.*

in|stall|ment plan /ɪnstɔ́lmənt plæn/ (**installment plans**)

NOUN An **installment plan** is a system in which the buyer can take and use goods by paying a percentage of the price as deposit, and pay the remainder due by a series of regular installments.

○ *If you, the customer, choose to pay for the goods under our installment plan, we, the seller, will remain the legal owner until the final installment is paid.*

○ *We offer installment plans to help customers who wished to buy a bag but cannot afford to pay in full.*

in|stall|ment sales /ɪnstɔ́lmənt seɪlz/

NOUN **Installment sales** are sales where fixed payments will be made regularly over a particular period of time.

○ *Taxes on installment sales are deferred until all payments are collected.*

○ *In installment sales, the purchaser agrees to pay for the purchase in a series of periodic payments.*

in stock /ɪn stɒk/

PHRASE When a physical or online store has an item **in stock**, it has that item in the store or in a warehouse and available for purchase now.

○ *All showers and enclosures in the range are held in stock and are available for fast delivery.*

○ *The toy store's website indicated that there were 10 of that particular teddy bear in stock.*

> **RELATED WORDS**
>
> The opposite of **in stock** is **out of stock**.
>
> ○ *Yes, that model of bed is definitely in stock.*
> ○ *I'm sorry to say that's out of stock.*

in-store /ɪn stɔr/

`GENERAL`

ADJECTIVE **In-store** is used to refer to activities or what is available in a department store or supermarket.

○ *The electronics retailer specializes in in-store demonstrations, which have increased both traffic and sales.*
○ *Loyalty cards offer regular customers discounts on everything they buy in-store.*

in|te|ri|ors /ɪntɪəriərz/

`PRODUCTS`

NOUN **Interiors** is the product category name for goods and design services for inside the home, including soft furnishings, wall and floor coverings, and lighting.

○ *She owns a successful design business that specializes in home staging, color consultation, and interiors.*
○ *Lighting has been the bestselling line in the interiors department.*

in|tern /ɪntɜrn/ (**interns**)

`PERSONNEL`

NOUN An **intern** is someone, often a young person, employed temporarily for work experience, but usually unpaid.

○ *The intern will gain hands-on experience in customer care and other customer-facing roles.*
○ *Gain retail industry experience and insight as an intern.*

in|ven|to|ry /ɪnvᵊntɔri/ (**inventories**)

MERCHANDISING

COUNT/NONCOUNT NOUN The **inventory** of a business is the amount or value of its raw materials, work in progress, and finished goods.

○ *Second-quarter growth slowed because distributors had too much inventory.*

○ *Piled-up inventories block working capital, and add to its costs.*

in|ven|to|ry ad|just|ment /ɪnvᵊntɔri ədʒʌstmənt/ (**inventory adjustments**)

MANAGEMENT ACCOUNTS

NOUN Inventory adjustments are increases or decreases made in inventory to account for theft, loss, breakages, and errors in the amount or number of items received.

○ *Inventory adjustments are increases and decreases made to inventory to match an item's actual on-hand quantity.*

○ *Inventory adjustments are corrections of inventory or stock records to bring them into agreement with the findings of the actual physical inventory.*

in|ven|to|ry cost /ɪnvᵊntɔri kɔst/ (**inventory costs**)

MANAGEMENT ACCOUNTS

NOUN Inventory costs are the costs to a business associated with holding stock, or money that is tied up in stock.

○ *By calculating the most economic order quantity the firm attempts to determine the order size that will minimize the total inventory costs.*

○ *The technique will help the manager compute the amount of stock to purchase with an order and so keep control of total inventory costs.*

in|voice¹ /ɪnvɔɪs/ (**invoices**)

SUPPLIER ACCOUNTS

NOUN An **invoice** is a document issued by a seller to a buyer that lists the goods or services that have been supplied and says how much money the buyer owes for them.

○ *The invoice will show the goods ordered and purchased, their quantity, their unit and total price, and any VAT being charged on the purchase.*

○ *Once the sales and marketing department allots the car, the finance department prints out the invoice for the dealer, and the car is delivered.*

---

in|voice² /ɪnvɔɪs/ (invoices, invoiced, invoicing)

Supplier accounts

VERB If you **invoice** a customer, you send or give them a bill for goods or services that you have provided them with.

○ *The agency invoices the client who then pays.*

○ *In industry, it is normal practice to invoice the customer and for the customer to pay the bill in due course.*

---

in|voice³ /ɪnvɔɪs/ (invoices, invoiced, invoicing)

Supplier accounts

VERB If you **invoice** goods that have been sold, you list them on an invoice.

○ *The bulk of cross-border sales are invoiced and settled in dollars.*

○ *Sales are recognized in the period in which they are invoiced.*

---

i|tem /aɪtəm/ (items)

Products

NOUN An **item** is a clearly identifiable product which can be given its own barcode.

○ *Customers with five items or less may use the express checkout.*

○ *Customers are no longer prepared to wait in line, especially for single purchases, and about a third will simply decide to buy the item at another store.*

Jj

jour|nal /dʒɜːrnᵊl/ (journals)

NOUN A **journal** is a book in which transactions are recorded before they are entered into a ledger.

○ *The journal shows all purchases, sales, receipts, and deliveries of securities, and all other debits and credits.*

○ *Transactions are periodically posted from the journal to ledger accounts.*

▶ **SYNONYMS:**
book of account
book of original entry
daybook

jun|ior sales as|so|ci|ate /dʒuːnyər seɪlz əsoʊʃiɪt/ (junior sales associates)

NOUN A **junior sales associate** is an inexperienced member of the sales staff, usually receiving training or supervised by more experienced staff.

○ *The junior sales associate works on the checkout counter, prices merchandise, and does general duties in the store.*

○ *We're looking to hire young people as junior sales associates to assist the existing sales team.*

just-in-time (ABBR JIT) /dʒʌst ɪn taɪm/

ADJECTIVE **Just-in-time** manufacturing or ordering methods avoid waste by producing or sending goods as they are needed rather than holding large stocks.

○ Just-in-time refers to inventory arriving or being produced immediately before shipment or the next process.

○ You should operate just-in-time ordering to improve stock turnover, and make sure you are continually shifting slow-moving or dead stock.

JV /dʒeɪ viː/ (short for **joint venture**)

DISTRIBUTION

ABBREVIATION A **JV** is a business activity in which two companies cooperate, sharing any risks and gains.

○ Businesses of any size can use JVs to strengthen long-term relationships or to collaborate on short-term projects.

○ The US-based retailer announced a new property JV in China which will see it invest in three shopping centers in the country.

j

Kk

---

ki|osk /kiɒsk/ (kiosks)

NOUN A **kiosk** is a small booth in the street or in a public place such as a railway station or airport, from which newspapers, hot drinks or fast food can be sold.

- ○ *I bought it at one of those kiosks selling perfume that pop up every Christmas in our local mall.*
- ○ *The grocery chain said that kiosks would be introduced into its supermarkets as part of its plan to develop the childrenswear trader through new channels.*

---

kit /kɪt/ (kits)

NOUN The **kit** in a store is the fixtures, fittings, and equipment that allow the store to operate efficiently.

- ○ *Once the painting is complete, the shelving, display cabinets, and fitting room kit can be brought in.*
- ○ *Store managers must make sure that there are no loose pieces of kit such as shelving lying on the shop floor.*

LI

---

lei|sure re|tail /ˈliʒər ˌriteɪl/

OUTLETS

NOUN **Leisure retail** is used to refer to retail outlets that attract shoppers to spend some of their free time browsing and shopping.

- ○ *Some of the most spectacular developments in Dubai are classed as leisure retail, with high-end brands and luxurious surroundings.*
- ○ *The focus is now on leisure retail, with shopping centers and malls designed to encourage customers to linger.*

---

life|style /ˈlaɪfstaɪl/

MARKETING

ADJECTIVE **Lifestyle** stores and products target customers who have a certain set of interests or want to live in a certain way.

- ○ *The retailer promotes itself as a lifestyle store catering to the needs of young do-it-yourself enthusiasts.*
- ○ *The mall is a unique mix of international fashion, arts and lifestyle brands, galleries and cafés, which will appeal to young image-conscious shoppers.*

▶ COLLOCATIONS:
lifestyle goods
lifestyle product
lifestyle store

LI|FO /ˈlaɪfoʊ/ (short for **last in, first out**)

MANAGEMENT ACCOUNTS

ABBREVIATION **LIFO** is a method of valuing inventory which assumes that the newest stock is sold first.

○ LIFO is not generally accepted as a suitable method of stock valuation because it does not reflect normal practice in which oldest stock is used first.

○ Using LIFO, the last costs of goods are recognized as costs first, leaving the oldest costs in the value of inventory.

---

light|ing /ˈlaɪtɪŋ/

PRODUCTS

NOUN **Lighting** is lamps, lights, or bulbs, or the area of a store where these items are sold.

○ Retail lighting must have good color, contrast, and balance.

○ Make sure all customer areas of the store have ample lighting with no dark corners.

---

like-for-like /ˈlaɪk fər laɪk/

MANAGEMENT ACCOUNTS

ADJECTIVE **Like-for-like** sales figures are based on a comparison with sales in the same period in another year.

○ Performance across all sectors improved as the month progressed, with overall like-for-like growth.

○ The company reported a 10.5 percent rise in like-for-like sales since the summer and a positive start for its new store format.

▶ **COLLOCATIONS:**
like-for-like decrease
like-for-like growth
like-for-like increase
like-for-like sales

---

line /laɪn/ (lines)

PRODUCTS

NOUN A **line** is one kind of product that a company makes or sells.

○ The company generally relies on a single vendor for order fulfillment with respect to each product line carried by the company.

○ The company is in the midst of a rebranding exercise, with new product lines and store fascias being introduced throughout its portfolio.

list price /lɪst praɪs/ (list prices)

PRICING

NOUN The **list price** is the price that the manufacturer of an item suggests that a store should charge for it.

○ *This is a small car with a list price of $18,000.*

○ *The new range of printers would have a list price between $1,700 and $2,000.*

▶ **SYNONYM:**
retail price

liv|er|y /lɪvəri/ (liveries)

MARKETING

NOUN A store or chain's **livery** is one or more features, such as color scheme, logo, layout, and staff uniform, that distinguishes it from other stores or chains.

○ *The chain carried out a comprehensive review of its entire image, from logos to packaging and the characteristic blue livery used for decades to identify its goods.*

○ *The orange and black company livery is a familiar one in shopping malls and retail centers country-wide.*

lo|ca|tion /loʊkeɪʃ°n/ (locations)

OUTLETS

NOUN The **location** of a store is the place where the store is situated.

○ *The type of retail location you choose for your store – a shopping mall, a strip plaza, or the downtown core – obviously has important consequences.*

○ *You may not see the company yet in Europe, although it has hundreds of locations in the US.*

lo|gis|tics /loʊdʒɪstɪks/

DISTRIBUTION

NOUN **Logistics** is the management of the flow of goods between point of origin and point of destination to meet customer and corporate requirements.

○ *Logistics encompasses all merchandise flows from manufacturer through the supply chain to the customer.*

○ *Firms are becoming smarter at maximizing logistics capabilities, such as sharing deliveries with other retailers, to reduce carbon emissions.*

---

loss lead|er /lɔs lidər/ (loss leaders)

PRICING

NOUN A **loss leader** is a product intentionally sold at a loss in order to encourage customers into a store or to a particular area of a store.

○ *A company offers discounts or temporarily sells a product below list price as a special event, sometimes even selling below cost as a loss leader.*

○ *Loss leaders are goods or services offered at steep discounts (generally below cost) in order to attract new customers to a store.*

---

loss|mak|er /lɔsmeɪkər/ (lossmakers)

MANAGEMENT ACCOUNTS

NOUN A **lossmaker** is any company, industry, or product that does not make a profit.

○ *Dairy farming would be a lossmaker without government subsidy.*

○ *It's important to identify lossmakers quickly and adjust your product range to focus on more profitable lines.*

---

loss|mak|ing /lɔsmeɪkɪŋ/

MANAGEMENT ACCOUNTS

ADJECTIVE **Lossmaking** businesses or business activities are losing money.

○ *They turned the discount chain from a lossmaking business into a very profitable one.*

○ *Lossmaking parts of the group will be closed down and the remainder sold off.*

---

loss pre|ven|tion /lɔs prɪvɛnʃən/

GENERAL

NOUN **Loss prevention** is any actions taken to reduce the amount of theft, breakage, or wastage in a business.

○ As the premier firm involved in retail loss prevention, we aim to equip our clients with an effective deterrent to theft and the ability to drive down the cost of crime.

○ Employee theft is a loss prevention area that generally doesn't receive as much monitoring as customer theft.

loy|al|ty /lɔɪəlti/

MARKETING

NOUN **Loyalty** is displayed by the customers of a store or chain if they visit more often and spend more money at that store or chain than they do at its competitors.

○ Customer loyalty exists when a person regularly patronizes a particular retailer that he or she knows, likes, and trusts.

○ Customers display a strong degree of brand loyalty by insisting on our products and accepting no substitute.

loy|al|ty card /lɔɪəlti kɑrd/ (**loyalty cards**)

MARKETING

NOUN A **loyalty card** is a card issued by a supermarket or chain store to a customer and used to record credit points awarded for money spent in the store.

○ The swipe card, which is also a loyalty card, automatically enters customers into the store's bonus system.

○ Loyalty cards offer regular customers discounts on everything they buy in-store.

Mm

mail or|der /meɪl ɔrdər/

DISTRIBUTION

NOUN **Mail order** is a system of buying and selling merchandise through the mail.

○ Another way to increase your sales volume is to use mail order and online shopping.

○ An emerging consumer trend shows that consumers are choosing to shop either online or by mail order.

Main Street /meɪn strit/

OUTLETS

NOUN **Main Street** is used to refer to the most important shopping street in the traditional center of towns and cities, and to the brand name stores typically found there.

○ Almost all the shops and restaurants along Main Street were shut for the season.

○ If you set up a store on Main Street, you choose when your store opens and closes, a freedom that you wouldn't have if based in a mall.

man|ne|quin /mænɪkɪn/ (mannequins)

STORE FIXTURES AND LAYOUT

NOUN A **mannequin** is a model of the human form used to display clothes in a store or in a store window.

○ If you're selling clothing, display it on a mannequin.

○ Using groups of mannequins in window displays will illustrate how combinations of clothing will look coordinated.

▶ SYNONYM:
dummy

mar|gin /mɑrdʒɪn/ (margins)

`PRICING`

NOUN A **margin** is the difference between the selling price and the cost of an item.

○ *Because the soft-drink bottler actually stocks the supermarket's shelves, store operators save on labor costs and generate very lucrative margins on soda sales.*

○ *There is no reason why we cannot improve our margins by focusing on our operational efficiencies.*

mark|down /mɑrkdaʊn/ (markdowns)

`PRICING`

NOUN A **markdown** is a reduction made in the usual price marked on a product.

○ *At $14.99 a bottle, it's not exactly cheap, but that's still a markdown from the $19 a bottle you'd pay buying direct from the winery.*

○ *The planned price reduction, or markdown, usually takes effect within a certain number of days after seasonal merchandise is received or on a specific date.*

m

mark down /mɑrk daʊn/ (marks down, marked down, marking down)

`PRICING`

VERB If you **mark down** something that you are selling, you reduce the selling price.

○ *Most supermarkets will mark down meat close to the sell-by date.*

○ *If a product is not selling, its price is marked down within a specified period.*

▶ **COLLOCATIONS:**
mark down a price
mark down a product

RELATED WORDS

The opposite of **mark down** is **mark up**.

○ *They listed the top 10 marked-up items in the grocery store.*

○ *Racks of clothing were all marked down by 10–50%.*

---

mar|ket¹ /mɑrkɪt/ (markets)

OUTLETS

NOUN A **market** is anywhere goods are exchanged for money, especially selling a certain type of merchandise, such as fish or Christmas gifts, or held by a particular group of sellers, such as farmers.

- *There is a farmers' market in the town every Friday.*
- *The Christmas market draws visitors to the city every year.*

mar|ket² /mɑrkɪt/ (markets)

MARKETING

NOUN The **market** for a particular product or service is all the people who buy it or might be persuaded to buy it.

- *For providing the supplier with a market for his goods, the small business normally receives a portion of the revenue on each item sold.*
- *New markets are opening up in the Far East and China.*

mar|ket³ /mɑrkɪt/ (markets, marketed, marketing)

MARKETING

VERB To **market** goods is to offer them for sale, or try to persuade people to buy them.

- *They have some imaginative ideas about how to market their restaurant in a bad economy.*
- *This marketing course will give you ideas on how to market your products.*

mar|ket|a|ble /mɑrkɪtəbᵊl/

MARKETING

ADJECTIVE **Marketable** goods are able to be sold because people want to buy them.

- *They must sell off the most marketable of the company's assets as quickly as possible.*
- *If the product is highly marketable, the manufacturer often can have their choice of several dealers in any one geographic area.*

mar|ket da|ta /mɑrkɪt deɪtə/

MARKETING

NOUN **Market data** is information gathered about the demand for goods, such as the number of units sold, and the value of goods sold.

○ *The magazine publishes retail industry news, retail jobs and key retail market data, from across the entire retail sector.*

○ *Retail market data is released at monthly intervals and gives a general picture of how the sector is performing.*

mar|ket|place /mɑrkɪtpleɪs/

OUTLETS

NOUN The **marketplace** is the commercial world of buying and selling.

○ *Even though online shopping will increase in popularity, physical stores will continue to fill a need in the marketplace.*

○ *With the advent of e-commerce and m-commerce, the retail marketplace is likely to look very different in 20 years' time.*

mar|ket re|search /mɑrkɪt rɪsɜrtʃ/

MARKETING

NOUN **Market research** is information gathered about what people want, need and buy, carried out by producers or sellers to help develop their business strategies.

○ *Recent market research supports this level of sales capacity.*

○ *Targeted market research will give retailers useful insight into their marketplace and their existing and potential customers.*

mark|up /mɑrkʌp/ (**markups**)

PRICING

NOUN A **markup** is a percentage that is added to the cost of a product, in order to cover costs and provide profit.

○ *The firm imports small appliances and sells them at a 10 percent markup.*

○ *The producer will allow the retailer to put on a markup to obtain profit, but the producers will not incur the distribution costs to the consumer.*

mark up¹ /mɑrk ʌp/ (**marks up, marked up, marking up**)

PRICING

VERB Retailers **mark up** a product when they add a percentage to its cost to cover their own costs and give them a profit.

○ *This is the standard percentage over cost that the store marks up an item.*

○ *Greetings cards are marked up by as much as 200%.*

▶ **COLLOCATIONS:**
mark up a price
mark up a product

mark up² /mɑrk ʌp/ (**marks up, marked up, marking up**)

PRICING

VERB To **mark up** goods is to increase their price.

○ *Some things tend to be marked up far more than they need to be when they're sold in stores – like overpriced veils at bridal salons.*

○ *Comparing the two stores showed how much goods may be marked up in the smarter part of town.*

▶ **COLLOCATIONS:**
mark up a price
mark up a product

mart /mɑrt/ (**marts**)

OUTLETS

NOUN A **mart** is a place or trading center where things are bought and sold.

○ *Older sales fleet cars are auctioned at the local auto mart.*

○ *Livestock producers can sell stock at the local auction mart.*

m-com|merce /ɛmkɒmɜrs/

GENERAL

NOUN **M-commerce** is the buying, selling, and ordering of goods and services using a mobile phone or other mobile equipment. The "m" in "m-commerce" stands for "mobile."

○ *Known as next-generation e-commerce, m-commerce enables customers to access the Internet without needing to find a place to plug in.*

○ *Its m-commerce application is expected to double the number of people accessing its online business via mobile handsets.*

---

mer|chan|dise¹ /mɜrtʃəndaɪz/

PRODUCTS

NOUN **Merchandise** is products that are bought, sold, or traded.

○ *Several stores have reported running out of merchandise.*

○ *Only a small percentage of merchandise is returned because of defects.*

---

mer|chan|dise² /mɜrtʃəndaɪz/ (**merchandises, merchandised, merchandising**)

MERCHANDISING

VERB To **merchandise** is to engage in the business of buying and selling goods.

○ *In some markets, the product is merchandised as a specialty item, while in others, it's sold solely on supermarket shelves.*

○ *Lighting control systems are merchandised along with the wide range of Christmas outdoor lights.*

---

mer|chan|dis|ing /mɜrtʃəndaɪzɪŋ/

MERCHANDISING

NOUN **Merchandising** is the selection, organization, and display of goods for sale in a retail outlet.

○ *Retail merchandising, in a nutshell, is selling and maintaining of products in a retail store.*

○ *She's responsible for the merchandising of the fullest possible range of products within a specified category.*

---

mer|chant /mɜrtʃənt/ (**merchants**)

PERSONNEL

NOUN A **merchant** is someone who owns or runs a store, or who buys and sells goods for profit.

○ *In a traditional retail transaction, the merchant typically makes contact with both the credit card issuer and the consumer.*

m

○ *The inventory management system helps merchants forecast consumer demand for merchandise based on historical sales data and fashion trends.*

mer|chant|a|ble /mɜrtʃəntəbəl/

GENERAL

ADJECTIVE If something is of **merchantable** quality, it is of high enough quality to sell or trade in.

○ *The customer was entitled to claim damages as the product was not of merchantable quality.*

○ *Something is of merchantable quality if it complies with all the appropriate standards applicable for products of that type.*

mer|chant ac|count /mɜrtʃənt əkaʊnt/ (merchant accounts)

CUSTOMER ACCOUNTS

NOUN A **merchant account** is a type of bank account that allows a company to accept credit cards.

○ *Getting a merchant account to handle credit card payments may be your best long-term solution to the problem of getting paid.*

○ *If you are taking credit card details over a website, you will need a merchant account with a reputable bank to process the payments.*

mer|chant fees /mɜrtʃənt fiz/

CUSTOMER ACCOUNTS

NOUN **Merchant fees** are money charged by a merchant service to a vendor for processing credit card transactions.

○ *Merchant fees are calculated as a percentage of each credit card sale.*

○ *The Director of Sales and Marketing said that credit card merchant fees were a significant and increasing cost to the company.*

mer|chant ser|vice /mɜrtʃənt sɜrvɪs/ (merchant services)

CUSTOMER ACCOUNTS

NOUN A **merchant service** is a provider of credit card processing services.

○ *In addition to banks, there are specific companies, often called merchant service companies, that offer credit card processing services.*

○ *The merchant service charge is a fee that retailers or merchants who accept Visa cards pay to their acquiring bank.*

---

min|i|mum or|der /mɪnɪməm ɔrdər/ (**minimum orders**)

DISTRIBUTION

NOUN A **minimum order** is the smallest amount or number that may be ordered in one delivery, usually to spread delivery costs over an economical number of units.

○ *There is no minimum order and all of our wholesale offerings are sold in small pack sizes, with delivery charged at cost only.*

○ *For orders of $200 or more, there's no delivery charge; for orders less than $200, the delivery charge is $12; and a minimum order of $40 is required.*

---

mod|el stock /mɒdəl stɒk/

MERCHANDISING

NOUN **Model stock** is the maintenance of adequate levels of stock of an item so that an adequate supply is always available for selling.

○ *Model stock is designed to assist in purchasing decisions and to ensure there is an adequate supply of merchandise on hand.*

○ *Model stock represents the highest inventory amount desired.*

---

mom-and-pop store /mɒm ənd pɒp stɔr/ (**mom-and-pop stores**)

OUTLETS

NOUN A **mom-and-pop store** is a small retail store owned and operated by members of the same family.

○ *Centralized markets, brand recognition, and industrially produced goods gradually undermined the position that local mom-and-pop stores enjoyed and placed it instead in the hands of manufacturers.*

○ *A common charge against big chains is that they put mom-and-pop stores out of business, but new businesses often cause the demise of old ones.*

move /mu̲v/ (moves, moved, moving)

MERCHANDISING

VERB To **move** merchandise is to sell it.

○ *In a recession, large department stores will have a difficult time moving products.*

○ *In the food court, managers aim to move product at its freshest rather than having any left at the end of the day.*

M|S|R /ɛm ɛs ɑ̲r/ (short for **magnetic stripe reader**)

PAYMENT TECHNOLOGY

ABBREVIATION An **MSR** is a device that converts information on the magnetic stripe of a credit card into data that can be understood by retail software.

○ *Cards typically include a magnetic stripe encoded with the unique ID number allowing them to be processed with a standard MSR device.*

○ *The MSR is a device that converts the information on the magnetic stripe of the credit card into computer-readable data.*

M|S|R|P (BRIT **MRP**) /ɛm ɛs ɑ̲r pi̲/

PRICING

ABBREVIATION **MSRP** is the manufacturer's suggested retail price, a price recommended for the sale of an item in all retail outlets.

○ *A vendor can require retailers to sell its products at the MSRP and refuse to sell its products to a discounter if they price products below it.*

○ *The dealer told me he could sell the new models at $250 off MSRP.*

mul|ti|pack /mʌ̲ltɪpæk/ (multipacks)

PRODUCTS

NOUN A **multipack** is a form of packaging that contains several units and is offered at a price below that of the equivalent number of separate units.

○ *For retailers, multipacks offer incremental sales and an escape from standard "3 for $1" pricing which often leaves the store with little if any profit.*

○ *In addition to different sizes, bottles and cans may be sold individually or as part of a multipack.*

mul|ti|ple store /mʌltɪpᵊl stɔr/ (multiple stores)

OUTLETS

NOUN A **multiple store** is one of several retail enterprises under the same ownership and management.

○ Multiple store operations have grown to the point that many retail firms operate in more than 100 locations.

○ The authority defines a multiple store operation as one having more than five stores.

mys|ter|y shop|per (also known as **secret shopper**) /mɪstəri ʃɒpər/ (mystery shoppers)

MARKETING

NOUN A **mystery shopper** is someone hired to pose as a customer and report on the quality of service received and how well a store or chain of stores is being run.

○ The mystery shopper poses as a normal customer and is given a specific task, such as purchasing a particular product or asking certain questions.

○ Mystery shoppers may check on any aspect of the customer experience, from sales presentations to how well displays are maintained to in-home service calls.

m

Nn

net¹ /nɛt/

ADJECTIVE The **net** amount of something is the amount that remains after subtracting taxes, expenses, losses, and costs.

○ *The sales figures are net of discounts, exclude sales tax, and are recognized at the time of sale.*

○ *The final figure for extraordinary losses was $3 million, net of $2 million in taxes.*

net² /nɛt/ (nets, netted, netting)

VERB If you **net** a certain amount that is the amount you are left with after subtracting costs.

○ *Profit margins were thin, with the company netting just $21.1 million.*

○ *The retailer netted $45 million on a turnover of $600 million.*

niche /niʃ/

ADJECTIVE **Niche** is used to describe products that appeal to a small, limited, or specialized group.

○ *The Jacuzzi began as a medical niche product before acquiring mass-market appeal.*

○ *Niche products, often sold through nontraditional channels, can demand a higher price.*

▶ **COLLOCATION:**
niche product

niche mar|ket /nɪʃ mɑrkɪt/ (niche markets)

MARKETING

NOUN A **niche market** is one in which there is a limited number of customers but those customers are prepared to spend money on the type of quality of product they want.

○ *To succeed in a niche market, you need a well-defined group of customers and products specifically tailored to their most urgent desires.*

○ *A niche market is a narrowly defined, specialized subject of interest that you can sell products into.*

non-food /nɒn fud/

PRODUCTS

ADJECTIVE **Non-food** items are those items that cannot be eaten but are commonly sold in food stores, such as cleaning products and toilet tissue.

○ *A high proportion of clothing, housewares, and other non-food retailers have been hit hard by the economic turndown.*

○ *The grocery giant is expanding its non-food range, concentrating on housewares.*

▶ **COLLOCATIONS:**
 non-food products
 non-food retailer
 non-food sales

nurse|ry /nɜrsəri/

PRODUCTS

NOUN **Nursery** is a retail product category for baby accessories, such as diapers and feeding bottles.

○ *We offer nursery products including Moses baskets, baby bedding, wooden stands, parasols, and cribs.*

○ *The store offers a baby shower list, so that friends and family can buy the nursery items the new parents need and want.*

Oo

of|fer¹ /ɔfər/ (offers)

PRICING

NOUN An **offer** in a store is an item that is reduced in price in some way, for example when you buy one, and get a second item at half price.

○ Our service will help you find the best of discounts and offers and so provide the correct boost for your business.

○ The store is having a sale and there are some fantastic offers.

RELATED WORDS

Note that a **BOGO** is an offer in which a customer receives an extra item of the same type, free or for a reduced price.

---

of|fer² /ɔfər/ (offers, offered, offering)

MERCHANDISING

VERB To **offer** goods is to present them for sale.

○ Vendors are able to offer lower prices on bulk purchases because the cost per unit is lower than for handling small orders.

○ We pride ourselves on offering our customers an unparalleled range of goods and superior service.

off-price /ɔf praɪs/

PRICING

ADJECTIVE **Off-price** retailers sell name brand or designer products at reduced prices.

○ Off-price retailers frequently price their merchandise 30 to 40 percent lower than their competitors.

○ Designer labels can often be bought cheaply at off-price retailers, who buy up out of season stock from the manufacturers.

---

on ac|count /ɒn əkaʊnt/

CUSTOMER ACCOUNTS

PHRASE You buy things **on account** when you buy them using a credit account with a supplier or store, and pay for them later.

○ The usual procedure for most businesses is to buy on account, rather than for cash.

○ If all, or a large part, of the overdue amounts are on account then you should obtain a list of the clients and start pushing for payment.

---

on con|sign|ment /ɒn kənsaɪnmənt/

SUPPLIER ACCOUNTS

PHRASE Goods from a supplier are **on consignment** when they are delivered to the retailer but paid for only after the retailer has sold them.

○ Goods are sometimes supplied on consignment, so that payment is not made until after the buyer has sold the goods, and in the meantime the goods remain the property of the supplier.

○ Some independent bookstores might be willing to accept a few books on consignment if they have the shelf space available.

---

on cred|it /ɒn krɛdɪt/

CUSTOMER ACCOUNTS

PHRASE Goods bought **on credit** are received now and payment for them is made later.

○ Accounts payable are amounts owed to others for goods or services purchased on credit.

○ No company will sell on credit without first evaluating the capability of the customer and his ability to fulfill the promise of paying the bills in time.

---

on hand /ɒn hænd/

MERCHANDISING

PHRASE Goods **on hand** are physically present, for example in a stock room or on display.

○ *Last week there were only 5 units, the last we had in stock, but I'll check if we have more stock on hand now.*

○ *Your chosen supplier should ideally have the merchandise already on hand in their warehouse and ready to send out as needed.*

---

on or|der /ɒn ɔrdər/

MERCHANDISING

PHRASE Goods that are **on order** have been ordered but have not yet been delivered.

○ *Merchandise that has been ordered but not yet received is on order.*

○ *Our new spring range is on order and is due to be in our stores next week.*

---

on sale /ɒn seɪl/

PRICING

PHRASE Goods that are **on sale** are for sale at a reduced price.

○ *The store has diversified, with a wider variety of products on sale.*

○ *The DVD of the film goes on sale today.*

---

on-shelf /ɒn ʃɛlf/

MERCHANDISING

ADJECTIVE **On-shelf** goods are available now and displayed for sale.

○ *With a refreshing new store design, we're seeing improved on-shelf displays.*

○ *They carry out on-shelf availability checks to see how well the supply chain is working.*

---

on the mar|ket /ɒn ðə mɑrkɪt/

PRODUCTS

PHRASE Something comes **on the market** when it is made available to be bought.

○ *The new smartphone has only been on the market for a week, and already more than 5 million units have been sold.*

○ *There are many credit card machines on the market and one will be suitable for your retail store.*

op|er|a|tions man|ag|er /ɒpəreɪʃənz mænɪdʒər/
(**operations managers**)

PERSONNEL

NOUN The **operations manager** in a store is the person responsible for the store's day-to-day working such as managing stock levels, manpower, display and advertising, and correct pricing.

○ *The operations manager will be responsible for conditions, safety, product levels, and cash handling procedures for several retail stores.*

○ *The operations manager ensures that store operations are efficient in terms of using as few resources as possible, and effective in meeting customer requirements.*

or|der¹ /ɔrdər/ (**orders**)

GENERAL

NOUN Someone's **order** is a usually written request to purchase the goods or services listed.

○ *There has been a rise in orders for spring season apparel.*

○ *The slump in the housing market held down orders for our kitchen cabinets and counters.*

or|der² /ɔrdər/ (**orders**)

PRODUCTS

NOUN If someone places an **order** for something, they ask that it be produced or supplied, in return for payment.

○ *One of the bigger chains has placed an order for 2000 units from the mill.*

○ *Within hours of you placing an order, the goods are dispatched from our warehouse.*

or|der³ /ɔrdər/ (**orders, ordered, ordering**)

GENERAL

VERB When you **order** something that you are going to pay for, you ask for it to be brought or sent to you.

○ *They are depleting their stock on hand before ordering new inventory.*

○ *Stores order their merchandise for the critical Christmas season in the summer.*

o

out|let /ˈaʊtlɪt/ (outlets)

OUTLETS

NOUN An **outlet** is a store, shop or other commercial establishment selling goods direct to the public, often from a single manufacturer or producer.

○ *Nearly all of its outlets, particularly those near shopping centers, now stay open until 8.00 p.m. six days a week.*

○ *A free-standing store is a retail outlet that stands by itself and is not attached to a mall or shopping center.*

out of stock¹ /aʊt əv stɒk/

MERCHANDISING

PHRASE When a store is **out of stock** of an item it normally keeps, it has none of that item available to buy now.

○ *The product was deleted from a retailer's order because the warehouse is out of stock.*

○ *It's frustrating when the item you have set your heart on is out of stock at your local store.*

out of stock² /aʊt əv stɒk/

MERCHANDISING

PHRASE When an item is **out of stock**, it is not immediately available for sale or use.

○ *They had sent the men's version of the sweater by mistake and it had been shipped from Iceland because it was out of stock in America.*

○ *The toy was so popular it was out of stock within a week.*

out-of-town /aʊt əv taʊn/

OUTLETS

ADJECTIVE **Out-of-town** stores or shopping malls are located outside the main central shopping area of a town or city and often having plenty of free car parking.

○ *Many customers prefer to drive to out-of-town retail developments, where parking is easier.*

○ *Many retailing activities changed location to out-of-town complexes because of the availability of large areas of unused land which was cheap in comparison to land within the town or city center.*

---

o|ver|age /ˈoʊvərɪdʒ/

MERCHANDISING

NOUN Overage is the term applied to the amount a physical inventory exceeds the book inventory.

○ *Even in well-managed businesses, a significant percentage of inventory is in overage at any given time.*

○ *Any significant overages or shortages in stock should be investigated.*

---

o|ver|buy /ˌoʊvərˈbaɪ/ (**overbuys, overbought, overbuying**)

MERCHANDISING

VERB When someone **overbuys**, they buy more of a product than they planned to buy or can sell.

○ *Merchandise jammed onto rails designed for fewer items is often a sign of someone overbuying.*

○ *An unseasonally warm winter can result in merchandisers overbuying coats and warm boots.*

> **WORD BUILDER**
> **over-** = too much
>
> The prefix **over-** often appears in verbs in which there is a sense of doing something more than usual or too much: **overbuy**, **overcharge**, **overstock**.

---

o|ver|charge /ˌoʊvərˈtʃɑrdʒ/ (**overcharges, overcharged, overcharging**)

PRICING

TRANSITIVE/INTRANSITIVE VERB If you are **overcharged** for something, you pay more than the correct price for it.

○ *The widespread use of scanner-based computer checkouts has led to increasing complaints of retailers overcharging their customers.*

○ *The customer was overcharged because the sales clerk scanned the item twice.*

> **RELATED WORDS**
>
> The opposite of **overcharge** is **undercharge**.

---

o|ver|stock¹ /oʊvərstɒk/ (overstocks)
GENERAL

NOUN An **overstock** is a situation where a store has more goods in stock than are required to meet demand.

○ *We have dedicated a portion of our showroom to seconds and overstocks, sold at discounted prices.*

○ *Off-price retailers frequently offer a high percentage of irregulars, overstocks, and out-of-season product.*

---

o|ver|stock² /oʊvərstɒk/ (overstocks, overstocked, overstocking)
MERCHANDISING

VERB When a company **overstocks**, it holds more of a product or products than it needs to satisfy demand.

○ *In some cases, companies overstocked due to purchases of goods which exceeded actual local requirements.*

○ *When inventory isn't moving or if you have overstocked a particular item, a loss leader can move it.*

---

own brand /oʊn brænd/ (own brands)
MARKETING

NOUN A supermarket's **own brand** is an item packaged and marketed under the brand name of the supermarket chain, rather than that of the manufacturer.

○ *There is also increasing competition from supermarkets' own brands, which are taking more shelf space.*

○ *Supermarkets' own brands often have cheaper packaging than branded items.*

own la|bel /oʊn leɪbᵊl/ (**own labels**)

NOUN An **own label** product is one that is produced for and stocked by a particular retailer and cannot be bought elsewhere.

○ *The company has established a retail network to market cotton men's and ladies' shirts under its own label.*

○ *The retailer's own label childrenswear is selling well, since it is good quality and affordable.*

o

Pp

pack /pæk/ (packs)

PRODUCTS

NOUN A **pack** is a small package, carton, or container.

○ *He bought two packs of cigarettes.*

○ *A blister pack is a package in which merchandise is covered with a transparent plastic casing and attached to a piece of card.*

pack|age /pækɪdʒ/ (packages, packaged, packaging)

PRODUCTS

VERB To **package** goods is to design and produce a container in which they will be transported and sold, especially when making them more attractive to customers.

○ *Cards are packaged with a backing and clear front to allow customers to see the product.*

○ *Simply put, an attractively packaged product is more likely to be purchased than one in a brown box.*

pack|ag|ing /pækɪdʒɪŋ/

PRODUCTS

NOUN **Packaging** is any outer layer, such as a carton or tray made of plastic or cardboard, used to protect products from damage and often printed with information about the product.

○ *This barcode must not have any hidden security numbers and should be placed on the bottom of the outer packaging of each unit.*

○ *Some supermarkets demand that new suppliers redesign their packaging and change how they handle shipping and inventory.*

pack|ing slip /ˈpækɪŋ slɪp/ (packing slips)

DISTRIBUTION

NOUN A **packing slip** lists the products included in a shipment.

○ When we write up the order, we write up the invoice for pricing, the packing slip for shipping the finished product, and the work order showing what needs to be done.

○ The document that tells the shipping department to release inventory for delivery is usually the packing slip.

pal|let /ˈpælɪt/ (pallets)

DISTRIBUTION

NOUN A **pallet** is a wooden platform on which goods are stacked and has two open ends that allow the entry of the forks of a lifting truck so the pallet can be lifted and moved about easily.

○ Our products originate from the catalogue companies who send us a wide variety of pallets packed with their customer returns, surplus stock, and clearance lines.

○ The automatic system identifies each load and moves the pallets to their allotted aisles in the warehouse.

pal|let|ize /ˈpælɪtaɪz/ (palletizes, palletized, palletizing)

DISTRIBUTION

VERB When a producer, wholesaler, or exporter **palletizes** goods, they stack or transport them on a pallet or pallets.

○ To maximize the use of container space, shippers routinely palletize cargo in container shipments.

○ Each load is palletized and wrapped ready for transporting to the docks.

pat|ron /ˈpeɪtrən/ (patrons)

SERVICE

NOUN The **patrons** of a store, hotel, or restaurant are its customers, especially those customers who visit regularly.

○ The food outlets and restaurants needed to tailor meals to patrons by researching their preferences.

○ In the survey, patrons of the restaurant can rate their levels of satisfaction about the food and drink they consumed and the service provided.

pay|ment /ˈpeɪmənt/ (**payments**)

CUSTOMER ACCOUNTS

NOUN You make a **payment** when you give a sum of money in exchange for goods you have received.

○ *As new electronic methods were introduced, a decline in the use of paper payment methods was observed.*

○ *There will be increased use of mobile devices to make payments for everyday transactions.*

Talking about payment

If payment is **authorized**, it is allowed by a bank.

If payment is **received** by someone, they are paid for something.

A **method of** payment is a way of paying for something.

---

pay-per-click (ABBR **PPC**) /ˈpeɪ pər klɪk/

PRICING

NOUN **Pay-per-click** is a system of payment used on the Internet in which an advertiser on a website pays the website owner according to the number of people who visit the advertiser's website.

○ *Pay-per-click is an Internet advertising model used to direct traffic to websites.*

○ *Pay-per-click is a faster way to boost traffic to your site than search engine optimization.*

pe|ri|od|ic in|ven|to|ry /ˌpɪəriˈɒdɪk ɪnˈvɛntɔri/ (**periodic inventories**)

MERCHANDISING

NOUN **Periodic inventory** is a method of valuing inventory, usually at the end of accounting periods, by physically counting all merchandise held in stock at that time.

○ *Periodic inventory does not maintain an ongoing record of all inventory items.*

○ *Periodic inventory does not have an accurate record of the inventories in between the inventory count periods.*

RELATED WORDS

Compare **periodic inventory** with **perpetual inventory** which is a method of stock control in which an accurate record of all merchandise bought and sold is available at all times.

---

per|ish|a|bles /pɛrɪʃəbəlz/

PRODUCTS

NOUN **Perishables** are goods that spoil quickly and therefore have a short shelf life, such as milk, bread, fruit, and vegetables.

○ *With a fleet of refrigerated trucks, the company is fully equipped to transport shellfish and other perishables.*

○ *Ports that handle imported food and other perishables need facilities like cold stores to keep the produce until it could be sold or processed.*

---

per|pet|u|al in|ven|to|ry /pərpɛtʃuəl ɪnvəntɔri/ (**perpetual inventories**)

MERCHANDISING

NOUN **Perpetual inventory** is a method of stock control in which an accurate record of all merchandise bought and sold is available at all times.

○ *Perpetual inventory reflects all known inventory adjustments as they happen, providing a more real-time, up-to-date inventory position.*

○ *A computerized system where each item of inventory is linked to the electronic accounting records is a perpetual inventory system.*

P

---

per|son|al shop|per /pɜrsənəl ʃɒpər/ (**personal shoppers**)

PERSONNEL

NOUN A **personal shopper** is a person whose job is to help people to choose their purchases, or to buy things on their behalf.

○ *Our free personal shopper service will help you find what you are looking for.*

○ *The store is trying to reduce the stress of festive shopping by appointing a personal shopper to customers who fill out a questionnaire.*

pet|ty cash /pɛti kæʃ/

CUSTOMER ACCOUNTS

NOUN **Petty cash** is money that is kept in the office of a company, for making small payments in cash when necessary.

○ *Staff refreshments for sales meetings are generally paid for from petty cash.*

○ *Companies normally maintain a petty cash fund to pay for small, miscellaneous expenditures.*

phys|i|cal in|ven|to|ry /fɪzɪkəl ɪnvəntɔri/ (**physical inventories**)

MERCHANDISING

NOUN To carry out a **physical inventory** is to count all the stock on hand.

○ *When a physical inventory is done, item costs must be learned, the quantity of every item in stock counted, and total inventory value at cost calculated.*

○ *Physical inventories are taken at least annually for all stores on a staggered basis throughout the year and inventory records are adjusted accordingly.*

pick /pɪk/ (**picks, picked, picking**)

MERCHANDISING

VERB To **pick** an item in a store or warehouse is to select it.

○ *He employs students to pick and pack the individual boxes of vegetables he sends out every week to his regular customers.*

○ *In the state-of-the-art warehouse, the automated grab picks the products to assemble each individual order.*

▶ **COLLOCATIONS:**
pick an item
pick goods
pick products

pick|ing tick|et /pɪkɪŋ tɪkɪt/ (**picking tickets**)

MERCHANDISING

NOUN A **picking ticket** is a list used for gathering items to be shipped from a store or warehouse.

○ *Picking tickets typically include item and customer information, where the item is physically located, quantity ordered, and a place to write the actual quantity of the item being shipped.*

○ *The picking tickets listing the items to be physically gathered for shipment are generated as soon as orders are received.*

PIN /pɪn/ (short for **personal identification number**)

PAYMENT TECHNOLOGY

ABBREVIATION Your **PIN** is the number, known only to you, that you type into card readers to confirm your identity when paying by credit or debit card, or when withdrawing money from an ATM.

○ *Sales clerks should always ask customers to enter their PIN when paying by credit card.*

○ *Please insert your card in the machine and key in your PIN.*

point of sale (ABBR **POS**, also known as **point of purchase**)
/pɔɪnt əv seɪl/ (**points of sale**)

MARKETING

NOUN A **point of sale** is the place in a retail store at which a sale is made.

○ *The point of sale can mean a retail shop, a checkout counter in a store, or any location where a sales transaction takes place.*

○ *A good point of sale system will replace older manual processes, keep all your information in one place for easy access and updating, and make ringing up sales much more straightforward.*

point-of-sale ter|mi|nal (ABBR **POST**) /pɔɪnt əv seɪl tɜrmɪnəl/ (**point-of-sale terminals**)

PAYMENT TECHNOLOGY

NOUN A **point-of-sale terminal** is any electronic device used to record and process information relating to sales.

○ *A point-of-sale terminal is a computerized replacement for a cash register.*

○ *Point-of-sale terminals to process credit-card transactions can be rented on a monthly basis.*

---

pop-up /pɒp ʌp/

OUTLETS

ADJECTIVE Pop-up is used to refer to stores and other small businesses that opened temporarily to take advantage of a trend or a seasonal or short-lived product, closing down when the selling opportunity has past.

○ *Temporary or pop-up stores are an increasingly popular marketing vehicle for generating publicity.*

○ *Pop-up stores spring up in interesting and unexpected locations, and do not need as much investment or polish as a permanent venture.*

---

pred|a|to|ry pric|ing /prɛdətɔri praɪsɪŋ/

PRICING

NOUN Predatory pricing is the practice of offering goods or services at such a low price that competitors are forced out of the market.

○ *Selling below cost to sell off excess inventory is not considered predatory pricing; selling below cost to drive out competitors is.*

○ *Mistaking competitive pricing for predatory pricing could inhibit healthy price competition.*

---

prem|is|es /prɛmɪsɪz/

OUTLETS

NOUN A company's **premises** is the land and buildings where it conducts its business.

○ *It is cheaper to sell online out of a warehouse than pay exorbitant amounts to rent retail premises.*

○ *There was a break-in at their premises and the thieves got away with jewelry worth more than $1 million.*

pre-sell /priːsɛl/ (pre-sells, pre-sold, pre-selling)

MARKETING

VERB To **pre-sell** a product to promote it with publicity before it comes on to the market.

○ They often pre-sell new titles by popular authors on their website before their release.

○ New generation smartphones are often pre-sold to customers eager to be ahead of the technological curve.

price¹ /praɪs/ (prices)

PRICING

NOUN The **price** of something is the amount of money that you have to pay in order to buy it.

○ Inflation is being pushed up by sharply higher prices for fuel and utilities.

○ There are still big variations in the prices charged for the same car model in different countries.

Talking about prices

If you make prices higher, you **increase** or **raise** them, and if you make them lower, you **cut**, **lower**, or **reduce** them. If you say that prices are **slashed**, you mean they have been cut a lot.

If prices are getting higher, you can say they are **rising** or **soaring**, and if they are getting lower, you can say they are **falling**. If you **quote** a price, you say you will do something or sell something for that price, and if you **charge** a price, that is how much someone must pay you.

If you decide how much things should cost, you **set** prices. If something is sold for a particular amount, it **fetches** that price. To talk about how much things cost, you can say that prices **start at** a particular amount, or that prices **range from** one amount to another. The **retail** price for something is the amount it costs in a store, and the **wholesale** price is the amount it costs to buy a large quantity of it.

P

price² /praɪs/ (prices, priced, pricing)

PRICING

VERB To **price** goods is to apply a price, or a price tag, to them.

○ It's unlikely that the new generation of phones can ever be priced below the $200 level that has spurred sales of earlier versions.

○ They came to the market with competitively priced clothing and footwear.

price break /praɪs breɪk/ (price breaks)

PRICING

NOUN A **price break** is a reduction in price, especially for bulk purchase.

○ Long lines are offputting to customers and even a price break is often not enough to convince them to waste that much time.

○ I tend to examine their clearance racks carefully, and ask if I can get a price break if I buy all the fabric left on the roll.

price check /praɪs tʃɛk/ (price checks)

PRICING

NOUN A **price check** is an investigation of the prices charged by different retailers for the same goods to find the best value.

○ Our price check survey, which compares 10,000 prices against our leading competitors weekly, shows that our price position has improved again.

○ All the major supermarkets use price checks to benchmark their pricing against their competitors.

price com|par|i|son /praɪs kəmpærɪsən/

PRICING

NOUN **Price comparison** is comparing the price of the same product in different outlets.

○ Price levels are based on price comparisons with major competitors.

○ Price comparison websites can take the hassle out of finding the best deal.

price-fix|ing /praɪs fɪksɪŋ/

PRICING

NOUN **Price-fixing** is the setting of prices by agreement among producers and distributors.

○ Horizontal price-fixing occurs when a group of competing retailers establishes a fixed price at which to sell certain brands of products.

○ There is a temptation for price-fixing among competitors to raise, lower, or stabilize prices.

price-sen|si|tive /praɪs sɛnsɪtɪv/

PRICING

ADJECTIVE A **price-sensitive** buyer is someone who is likely to stop buying a particular product if they think it is too expensive.

○ As initial sales slow down, the company lowers the price to draw in the next price-sensitive layer of customers.

○ The struggle to maintain the value of a brand while enticing the price-sensitive shopper needs to be carefully managed.

▶ **COLLOCATIONS:**
price-sensitive customer
price-sensitive shopper

price tag /praɪs tæg/ (price tags)

PRICING

NOUN The **price tag** on an article for sale is the label showing its price and other details.

○ The price tag on the garment said $50 but the price on the system was $47.

○ In the US, most consumers don't haggle and will simply pay the price on the price tag.

price war /praɪs wɔr/ (price wars)

PRICING

NOUN A **price war** is a period of intense competition between enterprises, especially retail enterprises operating in the same market, characterized by repeated price reductions.

○ *Even the world's most popular brands engage in regular price wars.*

○ *Cutting prices in an industry loaded with excess capacity may lead to price wars as competitors battle to hold on to market share.*

pric|ing gun /ˈpraɪsɪŋ ɡʌn/ (**pricing guns**)

PRICING

NOUN A **pricing gun** is a hand-held device used in stores for fixing a price label to a product.

○ *A handy item to purchase is a pricing gun, which is capable of mechanically printing your price codes on the price stickers.*

○ *Examples of retail store supplies your stockroom will need are pricing guns, labelers, and box cutters.*

pro|ceeds /ˈprəʊsiːdz/

MANAGEMENT ACCOUNTS

NOUN The **proceeds** is the money made from a sale.

○ *The company sold land to a developer and invested the proceeds in new outlets.*

○ *The property generates a good cash flow from the rental proceeds after deducting the monthly outgoings for maintenance and local rates.*

pro|ces|sor /ˈprɒsɛsər/ (**processors**)

MANAGEMENT ACCOUNTS

NOUN A **processor** is a company that processes payment transactions.

○ *If you are interested in upgrading to the latest card-reading machinery, you should contact your current credit card processor.*

○ *It links your POS system with most of the high-speed credit card processors in North America and internationally.*

pro|cure|ment /prəˈkjʊərmənt/

DISTRIBUTION

NOUN **Procurement** is the act or process of buying, including any negotiations that this involves on price and availability.

○ *The procurement process covers the subareas: contracting, purchasing, goods receipt, invoice verification, and creditor accounting.*

○ *The global retail sector's competitive environment requires today's retail procurement and supply chain professionals to improve efficiencies and reduce costs throughout their supply chain.*

prod|uct /prɒdʌkt/ (products)

PRODUCTS

NOUN A **product** is something that you manufacture or grow in order to sell it.

○ *This smartphone is one of the company's most successful products.*

○ *They sell most of their farm products to the larger supermarket chains.*

prof|it /prɒfɪt/ (profits)

MANAGEMENT ACCOUNTS

NOUN **Profit** is the amount of money you gain when you sell something for more than you paid for it.

○ *Overall sales have increased over the period, but profits are being squeezed by heavy discounting.*

○ *The growth stage is the stage of a product's lifecycle when sales rise rapidly and profits reach a peak, and then start to decline.*

prof|it cen|ter (BRIT profit centre) /prɒfɪt sɛntər/ (profit centers)

MANAGEMENT ACCOUNTS

NOUN A **profit center** is a part of a company that is responsible for its own costs and profits.

○ *Now that each profit center has to pay salaries, managers aren't so happy to take more workers than they need.*

○ *A profit center is an organizational subunit of a firm which is given responsibility for minimizing operating costs and maximizing revenue within its limited sphere of operations.*

prof|it mar|gin /prɒfɪt mɑrdʒɪn/ (profit margins)

MANAGEMENT ACCOUNTS

NOUN A **profit margin** is the difference between the selling price of a product and the cost of producing and marketing it.

○ *Profit margins measure how much a company earns in relation to its overall sales and, generally, the higher they are, the more efficient the company is.*

○ *Firms have tended to increase their profit margins on existing volumes, rather than cut prices to increase their market share.*

---

pro for|ma in|voice /proʊ fɔrmə ɪnvɔɪs/ (pro forma invoices)

SUPPLIER ACCOUNTS

NOUN If someone issues a **pro forma invoice**, they create an invoice before a formal order is placed or before the goods are delivered.

○ *Occasionally, a pro forma invoice is the first document to be sent by the seller in response to a buyer's request.*

○ *A pro forma invoice is just a more formal, detailed version of a quote and doesn't necessarily imply advance payment.*

---

pro|mo|tion /prəmoʊʃᵊn/ (promotions)

MARKETING

NOUN A **promotion** is something that advertises a product and helps to sell more of it.

○ *The retailer said it expected gross margins to be lower than for the previous year, due largely to an increase in clothing promotions.*

○ *Before committing yourself to a promotion, you need to be sure that it will increase sales and bring in new customers.*

---

pro|mo|tion|al code /prəmoʊʃᵊnᵊl koʊd/ (promotional codes)

MARKETING

NOUN A **promotional code** is a code offered by retailers to customers who can use it to receive a discounted price when buying products online.

○ *The website lists hundreds of voucher codes and promotional codes which means you can save money instantly.*

○ *Promotional codes can now be set to require other products in the cart to discount an item, or require that the user has previously purchased the item.*

pro|mo|tion|al e|vent /prəmoʊʃənᵊl ɪvɛnt/ (**promotional events**)

`MARKETING`

NOUN A **promotional event** is an occasion that draws attention to a particular product or products, such as a price decrease, or the chance to win a prize when buying the product.

- ○ Promotional events for our retail clients are held at some of the top conference and event venues and include tours and catering.

- ○ The in-store fashion show was the most successful promotional event that the store ran last year.

pur|chase¹ /pɜrtʃɪs/ (**purchases, purchased, purchasing**)

`GENERAL`

VERB When you **purchase** something, you buy it.

- ○ An experienced buyer can always negotiate price with potential suppliers on large orders of frequently purchased items.

- ○ The owner of a small fish market must purchase stock carefully to ensure a fresh inventory.

▶ **SYNONYM:**
  buy

pur|chase² /pɜrtʃɪs/

`GENERAL`

NOUN **Purchase** is the act of buying.

- ○ The best purchase price is the lowest price at which the owner can obtain goods and services of acceptable quality.

- ○ When small quantities of items are purchased infrequently, the small business owner must pay list price.

pur|chase³ /pɜrtʃɪs/ (**purchases**)

`GENERAL`

NOUN A **purchase** is something you buy.

- ○ If you find a fault with a purchase when you receive it, you should contact the seller immediately.

○ *The purchase of a ticket is a contract between the airline or tour operator and the person named on the ticket.*

---

pur|chase or|der (ABBR **PO**) /pɜrtʃɪs ɔrdər/ (**purchase orders**)
SUPPLIER ACCOUNTS

NOUN A **purchase order** is a written list of the goods or services that a person or company wants to purchase.

○ *Each fund reserves the right to reject any purchase order, and if a purchase is canceled because your check is returned unpaid, you are responsible for any loss incurred.*

○ *A purchase order is a written request to a supplier for specified goods at an agreed-upon price.*

---

pur|chase re|quest /pɜrtʃɪs rɪkwɛst/ (**purchase requests**)
MERCHANDISING

NOUN A **purchase request** is a document detailing required items, the number required and when they will be required. Once approved it becomes a purchase order.

○ *A purchase request is an unapproved purchase order.*

○ *The purchase request details what items and services are required, the quantity, supplier, and associated costs.*

P|V|V /pi vi vi/ (short for **PIN verification value**)
PAYMENT TECHNOLOGY

ABBREVIATION The **PVV** is the number encoded in the magnetic strip on the back of some types of debit or credit card, which allows the cardholder's PIN to be checked by ATMs and retail card readers.

○ *The PVV is the PIN number associated with check and debit cards.*

○ *The ATM or credit card reader will read the PVV before the payment is authorized.*

Qq

Q|R code /kyu ɑr koʊd/ (short for **quick response code**) (QR codes)

MARKETING

NOUN A **QR code** is a code containing information about an item, such as a description and the price, made up of a pattern of black squares or dots, which can be read and processed by a cellphone.

○ The QR code allows customers to rapidly access the product information from within the store as they examine the products by using their cellphone's camera to take a photo of the code.

○ The upmarket furniture specialist will use QR codes on tickets and advertising material, helping customers interact with the brand via smartphone technology.

quan|ti|ty dis|count /kwɒntɪti dɪskaʊnt/ (quantity discounts)

CUSTOMER ACCOUNTS

NOUN When you receive a **quantity discount** from a store or supplier, you pay less because you have bought a large quantity of goods. Also known as bulk buying discount.

○ Cumulative quantity discounts are offered if a firm's purchases from a particular vendor exceed a specified quantity or dollar value over a predetermined time period.

○ The retailer may receive quantity discounts from the supplier or manufacturer if its orders are large enough.

Rr

---

range /reɪndʒ/ (ranges)

PRODUCTS

NOUN The **range** available from a manufacturer, designer, or store is all the products they make or stock.

○ Online retailers can offer consumers a broader range of titles and information than bricks and mortar stores.

○ The manufacturer has the most comprehensive product range on the market.

> ### Adjectives used with "range"
>
> ○ They carry a **wide** range of electrical goods.
>
> ○ We stock an **extensive** range of Chinese brush painting art supplies.
>
> ○ Specialty stores, by their very nature, can offer customers a **broader** range of products.
>
> ○ We aim to offer the customer a **comprehensive** range of domestic cleaning products.

R

---

read|y-to-wear /rɛdi tu wɛər/

PRODUCTS

ADJECTIVE **Ready-to-wear** clothing is made in a series of standard sizes, rather than made to fit the exact measurements of individual customers.

○ In the ready-to-wear category, she wants to add even more prestigious international brands, a move that will put her in direct competition with other boutique owners on the street.

○ Clothing buyers attend all the ready-to-wear runway shows in spring and autumn to buy stock for the following season.

> **RELATED WORDS**
>
> The opposite of **ready-to-wear** is **custom-made** or **bespoke**.
>
> ○ *All our wedding gowns are custom-made to ensure perfect fitting.*
>
> ○ *We provide both ready-to-wear and bespoke suits for men who value classic tailoring.*

---

re|ceipt /rɪsiːt/ (receipts)

CUSTOMER ACCOUNTS

NOUN A **receipt** is a printed, or sometimes written, statement that shows that you have received goods or money.

○ *If you don't have a receipt, you can't return the item.*

○ *We require your email address, so that we can send you a receipt as soon as payment for the goods has been processed.*

> **PRONUNCIATION**
>
> Note the silent "p" in this word.

---

re|ceiv|a|bles /rɪsiːvəbᵊlz/

MANAGEMENT ACCOUNTS

NOUN **Receivables** are amounts of money owing to you that can be collected on.

○ *The group might have to write off as much as $200 million in bad inventory and uncollectable receivables.*

○ *In an effort to manage working capital better, the company is looking strictly at inventories, payables, and receivables.*

---

re|ceiv|er /rɪsiːvər/ (receivers)

SUPPLIER ACCOUNTS

NOUN A **receiver** is a document recording the quantity and condition of goods when they are received by the buyer.

○ *Invoices will not be approved for payment without a signed purchase order, packing slip, and signed receiver attached.*

○ *Before the receiver is signed, all merchandise must be inspected to verify that items being delivered are in good condition.*

▶ SYNONYM:
receiving report

---

re|fund¹ /rɪfʌnd/ (refunds, refunded, refunding)
CUSTOMER ACCOUNTS

VERB If someone **refunds** your money, they return what you have paid them.

○ *We will refund your delivery costs if the items arrive later than 12 noon.*

○ *We guarantee to refund your money if you're not delighted with your purchase.*

---

re|fund² /rɪfʌnd/ (refunds)
CUSTOMER ACCOUNTS

NOUN When you are given a **refund**, the money you have paid for something is returned to you.

○ *We will gladly collect the item back for free and give you a refund.*

○ *The customer may return any item in its original condition for a full refund.*

> **Verbs used with "refund"**
>
> ○ *I took the jacket back and they **gave/offered** me a refund.*
>
> ○ *If the radio doesn't work properly, take it back and **get** a refund.*
>
> ○ *If you are not completely satisfied with your purchase, please return it to us within 14 days to **receive/obtain/claim** a full refund.*

---

re|plen|ish /rɪplɛnɪʃ/ (replenishes, replenished, replenishing)
MERCHANDISING

VERB You **replenish** stock when you add more stock to fill empty or nearly empty shelves.

○ *When demand runs ahead of the anticipated usage rate, the owner can dip into the safety stock to fill customer orders until the stock is replenished.*

○ *Normally they do replenish their stock of out-of-stock items but the coat you wanted was in the end of season sale so you may not be able to get hold of it again.*

re|plen|ish|ment /rɪplɛnɪʃmənt/

MERCHANDISING

NOUN Stock **replenishment** is the process of adding more stock to replace what has been sold.

○ *The purchasers buy a certain quantity of the product, and when it is sold out, replenishment from the supplier takes place.*

○ *The replenishment rate depends on sales volume as well as consistency of supply.*

re|sale price main|te|nance (ABBR **RPM**) /rɪseɪl praɪs meɪntɪnəns/

PRICING

NOUN **Resale price maintenance** is a practice in which a manufacturer fixes the price for the resale of a brand product and the retailer is not allowed to sell it at a lower price.

○ *Manufacturers use resale price maintenance to more directly prevent inter-retailer price competition.*

○ *Resale price maintenance was an agreement between suppliers or manufacturers and retailers, restricting the price that retailers can ask for a product or service.*

re|tail¹ /riːteɪl/

GENERAL

NOUN **Retail** is the sale of goods individually or in small quantities direct to consumers.

○ *These days, retail is about so much more than merchandise. It's about casting customers in a story.*

○ *The world of retail is a fast-changing one and calls for constant evolution on the part of the retailer.*

re|tail² /riːteɪl/

GENERAL

ADJECTIVE If you talk about a **retail** business, price, or sale, you mean a business that sells goods directly to the public or a price or sale when you are selling goods directly to the public.

○ *Reimbursement will be the lower of either the retail price or the wholesale price plus $4.50.*

○ *Retail stores usually count on the Christmas season to make up to half of their annual profits.*

▶ **COLLOCATIONS:**
retail business
retail outlet
retail price
retail sale
retail store

---

re|tail³ /rı̱teıl/

GENERAL

ADVERB When goods are sold **retail**, they are sold in small quantities direct to consumers, usually from premises such as a store, shop, or boutique.

○ *Learn how to buy wholesale, sell retail, do inventory, and keep profit margins.*

○ *Growing numbers of retailers are launching Internet businesses, with selling retail online predicted to jump by 13% in the next year.*

---

re|tail⁴ /rı̱teıl/ (retails, retailed, retailing)

GENERAL

VERB A company or individual **retails** goods when they sell goods one at a time or in small quantities direct to consumers.

○ *The company produces and distributes sportswear which retails through department stores.*

○ *They are retailing the new model at $8.99.*

---

re|tail an|a|ly|tics /rı̱teıl æ̱nᵊlı̱tıks/

MARKETING

NOUN **Retail analytics** is any information that allows retailers to make smarter decisions and manage their businesses more effectively.

○ *Retail analytics can identify your best customers and where they live, and predict future spending in terms of amounts, categories, and even brands.*

○ *The company then applies a layer of predictive retail analytics to the response data, producing a view of consumer behavior, which retailers can use to sense product demand.*

re|tail an|chor /rɪ̱teɪl æ̱ŋkər/ (retail anchors)

OUTLETS

NOUN A **retail anchor** is a popular store whose name will attract customers to a shopping mall.

○ *A retail anchor store is a major retail store used to drive business to smaller retailers nearby.*

○ *These retail anchors are usually larger department stores or grocery stores which are the prominent businesses in shopping malls.*

re|tail price /rɪ̱teɪl pra̱ɪs/ (retail prices)

PRICING

NOUN **Retail prices** are the prices that the customers buying goods at retail outlets pay.

○ *Consumers respond to a lower retail price by switching their purchases of the manufacturer's product to the lower-priced retailer.*

○ *Additional markup is an increase in a retail price above the original markup when demand is unexpectedly high or costs are rising.*

re|tail the|a|ter (BRIT retail theatre) /rɪ̱teɪl θi̱ətər/ (retail theaters)

STORE FIXTURES AND LAYOUT

NOUN A **retail theater** is a display in a store that is very theatrical, artistic and creative, and deliberately designed to make shopping entertaining.

○ *That store is a good example of a retail theater. It describes itself as a theme park where customers are encouraged to buy souvenirs of their visit.*

○ *Retail theater is a concept sweeping through the retailing industry: by developing your services to delight your customers' five senses, you will see them return again and again.*

re|turn¹ /rɪtɜ̱rn/ (returns)

GENERAL

NOUN A **return** is an item that had been bought by a customer and is then brought or sent back to the store.

○ *Shoppers seem to have been impulse-buying and then thinking better of it, judging from the number of returns this week.*

r

○ *Depending on the store's return policy, it may be possible to offer in-store credit or gift cards instead of a cash refund.*

---

re|turn² /rɪtɜrn/ (returns, returned, returning)

GENERAL

VERB When you **return** faulty or unsatisfactory goods, you take or send them back to the store where you bought them.

○ *Have you read the notice saying you cannot return sale items?*

○ *The sales clerk should establish why the item is being returned by the customer. What is wrong with the item?*

---

re|turn on in|vest|ment (ABBR **ROI**) /rɪtɜrn ɒn ɪnvɛstmənt/

MANAGEMENT ACCOUNTS

NOUN A **return on investment** is a measure of profitability that is calculated by dividing net profit by total assets.

○ *Incentive plans are usually based on indicators of corporate performance, such as net income, total dividends paid, or some specific return on investment.*

○ *However large the potential return on investment, companies will find it hard to raise money for expansion.*

---

rev|e|nue /rɛvənyu/

MANAGEMENT ACCOUNTS

NOUN **Revenue** is money that a business receives.

○ *The company gets 98 percent of its revenue from Internet advertising.*

○ *They learnt how to project future revenue and profit estimates for the purpose of achieving steady growth.*

---

re|ver|sal /rɪvɜrsəl/ (reversals)

MANAGEMENT ACCOUNTS

NOUN A **reversal** happens when a buyer rejects or reverses a charge on their credit card, for example because they have not received goods ordered and the seller has not agreed to a refund.

○ *A reversal is available only to users who make a payment funded by their credit or debit card.*

○ *A reversal is when a chargeback is reversed and the funds are returned to the merchant.*

R|F|I|D tag /ɑr ɛf aɪ di tæg/ (short for **radio-frequency identification tag**) (**RFID tags**)

STORE FIXTURES AND LAYOUT

NOUN **RFID tags** are barcodes that make use of radio waves to send information tracking individual products at every stage, from delivery to stockroom to checkout, in a networked system.

○ *RFID tags have a computer chip that holds information, and a short- or long-range antenna that can send information back to a central processing unit.*

○ *RFID tags are used in the retail industry as a tracking device for inventory tracking from manufacture to distribution centers to the store.*

▶ SYNONYM:
smart label

---

ro|tat|ing stock /routeɪtɪŋ stɒk/

MERCHANDISING

NOUN **Rotating stock** is a system used especially in food stores and to reduce wastage, in which the oldest stock is moved to the front of shelves and new stock is added at the back.

○ *Stocking new merchandise behind or in place of old merchandise is known as rotating stock.*

○ *Rotating stock is moving older stock to the front of the shelf or display and placing newer stock, or stock that has just been delivered, behind this stock.*

R|R|P /ɑr ɑr pi/ (short for **recommended retail price**)

PRICING

ABBREVIATION The **RRP** of a product is the price that the manufacturer or wholesaler recommends that the retailer ought to charge for it.

○ *They were selling the goods at a promotional price of $2.99 instead of the RRP of $4.99.*

○ *The retailer offers savings of up to 60 percent off the RRP on great brands and labels.*

R|T|V /ɑr ti vi/ (short for **return to vendor**)

DISTRIBUTION

ABBREVIATION **RTV** is an instruction authorizing the return of unwanted or damaged goods to the seller, the cost of which will then be refunded to the buyer.

○ *The system simplifies outbound shipping from your stores, including RTV packages.*

○ *Merchandise will be inspected in order to extract damaged items under RTV agreements.*

R

Ss

sale¹ /seɪl/ (sales)

NOUN **Sales** of goods, property, or services is their exchange for agreed sums of money or credit.

- ○ *Sales of soft cheeses dropped by 2 percent.*
- ○ *Like-for-like sales of footwear grew 26 percent year-on-year.*

> **Talking about sales**
>
> Companies report that sales of a particular product have **risen** or **grown** when they have gone up. They say that they have **fallen**, **dropped**, or **slumped** when they have gone down.
>
> Something that causes sales to go up is said to **boost** sales.
>
> If a product is selling well, sales are **up**, **brisk**, or **booming** and if it is not selling well, sales are **down**, **flat**, or **sluggish**.

sale² /seɪl/ (sales)

NOUN If a store holds a **sale** it offers goods at reduced prices, usually to clear old stocks.

- ○ *At the local shopping mall the winter sales were still in full swing in early February.*
- ○ *Just after Thanksgiving, Black Friday is the day of sales that is supposed to get retailers back "into the black."*

S

sale|a|ble /seɪləbᵊl/

MERCHANDISING

ADJECTIVE **Saleable** items are suitable for selling or capable of being sold.

○ Returns of merchandise will be permitted only if presented in saleable condition accompanied by the original sales receipt.

○ Even stock that does not have a shelf life should be checked for condition and soiling of labels to ensure that it is in a saleable condition.

sale or re|turn /seɪl ər rɪtɜrn/

SERVICE

PHRASE **Sale or return** is an arrangement by which a retailer pays only for goods sold, returning those that are unsold to the wholesaler or manufacturer.

○ Sale or return agreements allow the retailer to return unsold stock, thus eliminating write-offs.

○ In tough economic times, sale or return may be the only option you have to place your goods with a retailer.

sales as|so|ci|ate /seɪlz əsoʊʃiɪt/ (**sales associates**)

PERSONNEL

NOUN A **sales associate** is someone who sells goods or services in a store, often stationed behind a counter.

○ Inexperienced or poorly trained sales associates are happy when a customer simply makes a buying decision without their input.

○ Sales associates and customer service teams should approach each customer encounter as one element in a multi-faceted relationship.

sales clerk (ABBR **clerk**) /seɪlz klɜrk/ (**sales clerks**)

PERSONNEL

NOUN A **sales clerk** is someone who sells goods in a store.

○ A sales clerk runs a cash register, provides customer service, and helps keep the store clean.

○ As sales clerks often remove items from hangers, there should be a neat and organized space at the checkout counter for these hangers.

sales com|mis|sion /seɪlz kəmɪʃᵊn/

SERVICE

NOUN **Sales commission** is the percentage of the value of a sale that a sales associate or sales representative may earn.

○ Variable costs include your cost of goods sold, credit card fees, shipping costs and sales commission you may pay to sales staff.

○ Should sales commission be a percentage of sales or a percentage of gross profit from the item?

sales fore|cast /seɪlz fɔrkæst/ (**sales forecasts**)

MARKETING

NOUN A **sales forecast** is a prediction of future sales of a product, either based on previous sales patterns or judgements about new markets and other likely factors.

○ Sales forecasts are notoriously unreliable, for actual sales depend in part upon factors that lie outside the control of the firm.

○ Sales forecasts for the coming six months are downbeat.

sales man|ag|er /seɪlz mænɪdʒər/ (**sales managers**)

PERSONNEL

NOUN A **sales manager** is a manager responsible for the sales area in a store, including the supervision of sales associates and other employees.

○ If sales are slow during the month, sales managers will know immediately and can then take proactive measures.

○ The sales manager liaises with the purchasing manager to keep shelves stocked and displays fresh.

sales pitch /seɪlz pɪtʃ/ (**sales pitches**)

SERVICE

NOUN A **sales pitch** is a persuasive argument used in selling.

○ An effective sales pitch gets your customer's attention and builds interest and excitement about the product.

○ If all you ever do is make a sales pitch or talk about your store, your customers will quickly stop reading and start deleting your email messages.

sales rep|re|sent|a|tive (ABBR **sales rep**) /seɪlz rɛprɪzɛntətɪv/ (**sales representatives**)

PERSONNEL

NOUN A **sales representative** is a person who sells products on behalf of a company, usually traveling away from their own company's premises to find and sell to customers.

○ *Too often, business owners send sales representatives out into the field with little or no training and then wonder why they cannot produce.*

○ *Sales representatives follow up leads from clients, participate in trade shows and exhibitions, and may visit new clients unannounced.*

sales slip /seɪlz slɪp/ (**sales slips**)

SERVICE

NOUN A **sales slip** is a piece of paper that you are given when you buy something in a store, which shows when you bought it and how much you paid.

○ *The sales clerk was happy to exchange an item for any customer who had retained their sales slip.*

○ *If you want to return merchandise to the store, the staff will insist on seeing the original sales slip.*

sales tax /seɪlz tæks/

MANAGEMENT ACCOUNTS

NOUN **Sales tax** is a government tax on each item sold.

○ *Sales taxes vary according to the taxable status of the merchandise and customer and can differ according to location.*

○ *The 4 percent sales tax went into effect October 1st in an attempt to collect more revenue to help close the budget gap.*

sam|ple /sæmpəl/ (**samples**)

PRODUCTS

NOUN A **sample** is a small quantity of a product, given free so that customers can try it or examine it before making the decision to buy.

○ *At the deli, there are always free samples of cured meats and cheeses.*

○ *You will often get free samples at the cosmetics counter, and sometimes a free makeover is offered.*

scan|ner /skǽnər/ (**scanners**)

PAYMENT TECHNOLOGY

NOUN A **scanner** is a machine that reads electronic barcodes.

○ *The unit is a hand-held scanner used to scan the tag or barcode on a product.*

○ *It was one of the first retailers to make handheld scanners available to customers, allowing them to pay at self-service checkouts.*

sea|son /sízᵊn/ (**seasons**)

PRODUCTS

NOUN In retailing, a **season** is a distinct time of the year when certain types of goods are available or in vogue.

○ *We will also open a new store this year in the St. Louis market in time for the back-to-school selling season.*

○ *Spring season fashions are bought the previous summer or fall.*

sea|son|al /sízənᵊl/

PRODUCTS

ADJECTIVE **Seasonal** items are available only during certain seasons, or vary with the seasons.

○ *He does an analysis of daily, weekly, or monthly figures to evaluate the degree to which seasonal factors influence sales.*

○ *The company was affected by the miserable summer weather and the warm fall conditions, but such unusual conditions will always impact seasonal products.*

▶ **COLLOCATIONS:**
seasonal product
seasonal sales

sea|son|al pro|mo|tion /sízənᵊl prəmóuʃᵊn/ (**seasonal promotions**)

MARKETING

NOUN **Seasonal promotions** are items marketed to customers at the appropriate time of year, such as coats in the winter and bathing suits in the summer.

○ *The sales team is focusing on seasonal promotions for Halloween and Christmas.*

○ *If you're thinking about fall seasonal promotions, consider sponsoring your local fall festival.*

---

se|conds /sɛkəndz/

PRODUCTS

NOUN **Seconds** are goods that are not top quality, either because they are flawed or last season's.

○ *Stores known as off-price retailers buy manufacturers' seconds, overruns, returns, and off-season merchandise for resale to consumers at deep discounts.*

○ *Seconds are items with definite defects which prevent the manufacturer from selling them to their first-line customers.*

> **RELATED WORDS**
>
> Compare **seconds** with **firsts** which are saleable goods of the highest quality.

---

se|cu|ri|ty guard /sɪkyʊərɪti gɑrd/ (**security guards**)

PERSONNEL

NOUN A **security guard** is someone who watches for thieves in stores and prevents shoplifting.

○ *The single diamond, costing $2 million, is on display in the window and security guards prowl the entrances.*

○ *Uniformed security guards are a powerful deterrent to shoplifters.*

---

se|cu|ri|ty man|ag|er /sɪkyʊərɪti mænɪdʒər/ (**security managers**)

PERSONNEL

NOUN The **security manager** of a store is the person responsible for organizing all security in the store and to whom security guards report.

○ *Our security manager examines the key techniques involved in identifying and managing loss in our retail outlets.*

○ *The store's security manager coordinates store detectives and security guards.*

se|lec|tion /sɪlɛkʃ°n/ (**selections**)

PRODUCTS

NOUN The **selection** in a store is the choice or range of goods available to customers of that store.

○ *The online store offers a broad selection of music CDs, concert tickets, and other music-related products.*

○ *We offer a wide selection of gifts and greetings cards.*

---

self-check|out /sɛlf tʃɛkaʊt/ (**self-checkouts**)

STORE FIXTURES AND LAYOUT

NOUN A **self-checkout** is a checkout where customers scan, pack and pay for their goods in a store without being served by a sales associate.

○ *Self-checkout has reduced waiting times and improved customer flow.*

○ *A staff member is always on hand in case customers experience any problems with self-checkout.*

---

sell-by date /sɛl baɪ deɪt/ (**sell-by dates**)

PRODUCTS

NOUN The **sell-by date** is printed on the packaging of food and other perishables to indicate the date after which that item should not be offered for sale.

○ *Once food reaches its sell-by date, it's thrown away, but it's not as if that date is magic and the food will instantly spoil at midnight.*

○ *Grocery retailers cannot display goods that are past their sell-by date.*

> **RELATED WORDS**
>
> Compare **sell-by date** with **use-by date** which is the last date recommended by the manufacturer or producer on which the product should be eaten or otherwise used.

---

sell in /sɛl ɪn/ (**sells in, sold in, selling in**)

PRODUCTS

VERB When a manufacturer or producer **sells in** new products to a retail outlet they are available to the public from that outlet.

○ *Ideally, what is sold in should equal sell through.*

○ *Suppliers selling in to the grocery giant benefit from volume sales.*

---

sell off /sɛl ɔf/ (sells off, sold off, selling off)

MERCHANDISING

VERB To **sell off** things left in stock is to get rid of them, usually by selling them at very low prices.

○ *When they renew their range annually, they sell off their end-of-line stock.*

○ *Following poor group results, the chain sold off some of its less profitable stores.*

---

sell out /sɛl aʊt/ (sells out, sold off, selling off)

MERCHANDISING

VERB If a store **sells out of** a product, it sells its entire stock leaving none for customers to buy.

○ *The clerk politely explained that they had sold out of the item and that the manufacturers had been particularly slow in delivering more stock.*

○ *Within twenty-four hours of the item going on sale, it had sold out at every local outlet.*

---

sell-through /sɛl θru/

MERCHANDISING

NOUN **Sell-through** is the ratio of goods sold by a retailer to the quantity originally delivered to the retailer from wholesale.

○ *Sell-through is the amount of merchandise that is actually bought by end users.*

○ *The sell-through rate can vary according to the time of year, and even the weather.*

---

se|ri|al num|ber /sɪəriəl nʌmbər/ (serial numbers)

GENERAL

NOUN The **serial number** on a product is the unique number that identifies it from others of the same type made by the same manufacturer.

○ *I can't find a serial number anywhere on the outside of the machine.*

○ *Technical support will need the serial number, which can usually be found on the base of the machine.*

shelv|ing u|nit /ʃɛlvɪŋ yunɪt/ (**shelving units**)

STORE FIXTURES AND LAYOUT

NOUN A **shelving unit** is a flexible display system which can be moved and adjusted to accommodate different product dimensions.

○ *A gondola is an island shelving unit open on two sides.*

○ *The top shelf over a shelving unit, known as a riser, is used to house overstocks.*

ship /ʃɪp/ (**ships, shipped, shipping**)

DISTRIBUTION

VERB When goods that have been ordered are **shipped**, they are sent out, by sea, air, train, or road, by a supplier for delivery to the customer.

○ *Products will typically be shipped within two business days after an order is placed and confirmation will be provided via e-mail.*

○ *We will send you an email when your order is shipped from our warehouse.*

ship|ment /ʃɪpmənt/ (**shipments**)

DISTRIBUTION

COUNT/NONCOUNT NOUN A **shipment** is all of the goods being shipped together at the same time.

○ *Risk of loss passes from the manufacturer as soon as the carrier takes possession of the shipment.*

○ *After that, food shipments to the port could begin in a matter of weeks.*

ship|per /ʃɪpər/ (**shippers**)

DISTRIBUTION

NOUN **Shippers** are businesses that transport goods, especially those concerned with exporting and importing.

○ *The freight forwarder combines small shipments from different shippers into larger shipments.*

○ *A pickup order is a request by a shipper or consigner to pick up goods to be transported at a specific location on a specific date and time.*

ship|ping doc|u|ments /ˈʃɪpɪŋ ˈdɒkyəmənts/

| DISTRIBUTION |

NOUN **Shipping documents** are forms that accompany a shipment listing the date shipped, the customer, the method of shipment, and the quantities and specifications of goods shipped.

○ *Shipping documents usually include bills of lading, packing lists, invoices, insurance documents, and air waybills.*

○ *Exporters should submit shipping documents along with declaration forms duly signed by customs within 21 days from the date of exports.*

shop /ʃɒp/ (shops)

| OUTLETS |

NOUN A **shop** is a small retail outlet where goods and services are offered for sale.

○ *She runs a cake shop, catering children's birthday parties and weddings.*

○ *Children love the old-fashioned candy shop with its jars and brightly colored wares.*

shop floor /ʃɒp flɔr/

| STORE FIXTURES AND LAYOUT |

NOUN The **shop floor** is the area of a store that is accessible by the public, excluding storerooms, stockrooms, and offices.

○ *The shop floor is the location in a retail store where goods are displayed and sales transactions take place.*

○ *The company has an intensive training program which is intended to give new employees the capability to move from the shop floor into retail management.*

PARTS OF A STORE

The following are all areas of a store, each with a different function:

bargain basement
an area or floor below the first floor of a department store where goods are sold at reduced prices

checkout counter
a place in a store where customers go to pay for the goods they want to buy

fascia
any surface on the outside of the shop or store that displays the company name, company logo, and company color scheme

fitting room
a cubicle for customers to use when trying on clothes, usually having mirrors and separate female and male sections

stockroom
a room in a store in which a stock of goods is kept

store front
the window of a store that can be looked into from the street, often displaying the types of product the store sells

window display
a display in a store front showing examples of the goods sold in that store

---

shop-in-shop /ʃɒp ɪn ʃɒp/ (shops-in-shop)

OUTLETS

NOUN A **shop-in-shop** is an area that one retailer sublets within another retailer's premises.

○ *The majority of perfume sales are made through shop-in-shop points rather than standalone stores.*

○ *The CEO expects that in partnership with large department stores the company will eventually boast 50 or 60 shops-in-shop promoting the brand.*

---

shop|keep|er /ʃɒpkipər/ (shopkeepers)

PERSONNEL

NOUN A **shopkeeper** is someone who owns or manages a shop or small store.

○ *Generally, shop employees are not shopkeepers, but are often incorrectly referred to as such.*

○ *Local shopkeepers are worried about the rise in petty theft and shoplifting.*

S

shop|ping bag /ˈʃɒpɪŋ bæg/ (shopping bags)

GENERAL

NOUN A **shopping bag** is a paper or plastic bag supplied by a store to a customer for carrying away purchases.

○ Reusable shopping bags are more eco-friendly than plastic.

○ On Black Friday, the first 300 shoppers get free whatever they can fit into their shopping bags.

shop|ping cen|ter (BRIT shopping centre) /ˈʃɒpɪŋ sɛntər/ (shopping centers)

OUTLETS

NOUN A **shopping center** is a specially-built area containing a lot of different stores.

○ Neighborhood shopping centers usually consist of several small convenience and specialty stores.

○ Shoppers are using out-of-town shopping centers and supermarkets in search of cheaper prices.

shop|ping mall (ABBR mall) /ˈʃɒpɪŋ mɔl/ (shopping malls)

OUTLETS

NOUN A **shopping mall** is a large enclosed shopping center.

○ The 50s saw the emergence of the enclosed shopping mall, providing an end-to-end shopping and entertainment experience from food courts and theaters to shopping outlets.

○ In a deal worth $170 million, shopping malls will be opened in three Chinese cities, each of which will include a hypermarket as the anchor tenant.

short or|der /ˈʃɔrt ɔrdər/ (short orders)

MERCHANDISING

NOUN If you receive a **short order**, the number of items you receive is below the number you ordered.

○ A miskeying of the figure 3 for a 5 had resulted in several short orders, which delayed customer deliveries.

○ A short order from the factory meant that not all customer orders could be fulfilled.

show|room /ʃoʊrʊm/ (showrooms)

OUTLETS

NOUN A **showroom** is a room or other enclosed area used to display a company's products.

○ *These kitchen cabinets and counters are available for order at any of our showrooms.*

○ *A typical car dealership sells used cars outside, with new cars in the showroom.*

shrink|age /ʃrɪŋkɪdʒ/

MERCHANDISING

NOUN In a retail store, **shrinkage** is the loss of merchandise through theft or damage.

○ *Shrinkage is due to shoplifting losses, breakage, and accounting errors.*

○ *The average shrinkage percentage through theft in the retail industry is about 2% of sales.*

side|line /saɪdlaɪn/ (sidelines)

OUTLETS

NOUN A **sideline** is a business activity carried on at the same time, by the same person, or at the same premises, as another, more important, business activity.

○ *The garden center developed a lucrative sideline, supplying floral displays to corporate events.*

○ *Green energy could be a profitable sideline for businesses willing to rent out their roof space for solar panels.*

sign|age /saɪnɪdʒ/

MARKETING

NOUN **Signage** is any printed material in a store that guides or informs customers, such as posters.

○ *The value-for-money theme can be included in store signage, window displays, and impact displays within the store.*

○ *In large stores in particular, signage is required to help customers locate the merchandise that they are looking for.*

sign|post|ing /ˈsaɪnpoʊstɪŋ/

STORE FIXTURES AND LAYOUT

NOUN **Signposting** is the way customers are led through a store to make sure they see as much as possible. It may include floor plans, signs on walls, or arrows on floors.

○ *Promotions and meal deals are key to maximizing sales of the chilled category, and effective signposting will ensure the shopper is aware that chilled products are stocked.*

○ *Signposting in larger shopping centers is very important: the design and direction must be clear and unambiguous, to help people find their destination.*

SKU /ˌskjuː/ (short for **stock-keeping unit**)

MERCHANDISING

ABBREVIATION An **SKU** is a unique number given to a product so that it can be identified using retail software. A product's SKU may be linked to its barcode.

○ *The bar-coded labels complement the SKU numbers most retailers currently use to track inventory.*

○ *The retailer wanted to eliminate one SKU from his inventory to make room for a betterselling product.*

slat|wall mer|chan|dis|er /ˈslætwɔl ˈmɜrtʃəndaɪzər/ (**slatwall merchandisers**)

STORE FIXTURES AND LAYOUT

NOUN A **slatwall merchandiser** is a three-dimensional display unit with grooves cut into its surface into which metal hanging rails can be fixed at various heights.

○ *Cards can be displayed on a freestanding slatwall merchandiser which is readily adaptable using standard hooks, prongs, and arms.*

○ *Slatwall merchandisers that customers can walk around and floor displays located around the shop floor enhance the complete look of your retail store.*

slat|wall pan|el /ˈslætwɔl ˈpænəl/ (**slatwall panels**)

STORE FIXTURES AND LAYOUT

NOUN A **slatwall panel** is a slatted surface which can be fixed to the wall from which shelves or hooks can be hung at varying heights to display merchandise.

○ *Manufactured from medium-density fiberboard, slatwall panels can be fitted to walls or used in mid-floor displays.*

○ *Slatwall panels make good use of available wall space, and can be used to display many types of merchandise.*

---

small-for|mat /smɔl fɔrmæt/

OUTLETS

ADJECTIVE A **small-format** store is one in which a large retail chain offers only part of their range in a smaller store.

○ *The luxury department store is to open its first small-format store in the new downtown mall.*

○ *Small-format stores attract the 25 to 35 years demographic better than out-of-town stores because they resonate with the young urban lifestyle of picking up goods in town on the way home from work.*

---

soft fur|nish|ings /sɔft fɜrnɪʃɪŋz/

PRODUCTS

NOUN **Soft furnishings** is a product category name for items made from fabric such as curtains, cushions, and bedding.

○ *We are one of the country's largest homeware and soft furnishings stores, selling bedding, curtains, and blinds.*

○ *All soft furnishings including drapes, blinds, cushions, bedding, and table linen are on sale this week.*

---

soft sell /sɔft sɛl/

GENERAL

NOUN If a salesman uses the **soft sell**, he or she tries to sell you something using indirect methods.

○ *The soft sell first explores the customer's needs and wants, through probing questions and careful listening.*

○ *What you won't get is a hard sell – rather the art of the soft sell is back. If you look as if you want to be left alone to browse, you will be.*

spe|cial or|der /spɛʃ³l ɔrdər/ (**special orders**)

SERVICE

NOUN A **special order** is an extra order or an order for an item specially requested by a customer.

○ If the item is not one you normally carry, can you send a special order to the supplier?

○ Special orders for non-stock products are processed efficiently, using automated procedures, and quickly directed to the relevant supplier.

spot light|ing /spɒt laɪtɪŋ/

MERCHANDISING

NOUN **Spot lighting** is lighting directed towards and used to draw attention to a product or display.

○ Spot lighting draws the customer's eye to the center of the display.

○ Clever use of spot lighting will attract customers to high-value items.

stand|ard cost /stændərd kɒst/ (**standard costs**)

MANAGEMENT ACCOUNTS

NOUN A **standard cost** is the budgeted cost of a regular manufacturing process against which actual costs are compared.

○ Of course, if a new product, service, or process is to be carried out, the initial standard costs will have to be estimated.

○ Factory variance is the difference between product transferred at standard cost, and production at actual cost.

stock /stɒk/

MERCHANDISING

NOUN A store's **stock** is the goods that it has available to sell.

○ The buyer ordered $27,500 worth of stock.

○ Most of the store's stock was destroyed in the fire.

> The following are words connected with managing stock levels:
>
> barcode, clearance, destock, EPOS, periodic inventory, perpetual inventory, physical inventory, replenish, replenishment, VMI

stock al|lo|ca|tion /stɒk æləkeɪʃᵊn/

MERCHANDISING

NOUN **Stock allocation** is the decisions made about how quantities held at a central point will be distributed amongst several outlets in a retail chain.

○ *The software deals with stock allocation whether you are fulfilling sales orders or carrying out branch stock replenishment.*

○ *Stock allocation is about ensuring that the right stock is available at the right time in each of the retailer's outlets.*

stock|ing u|nit /stɒkɪŋ yunɪt/ (**stocking units**)

MERCHANDISING

NOUN A **stocking unit** is a measurement or number by which items are kept in inventory, for example by dozens, kilograms, or cases.

○ *The stocking unit in your store for an item might be "each," but you might receive an item from your vendor by the alternate unit "case."*

○ *This is the price per stocking unit, i.e. the unit in which you store the item.*

stock or|der /stɒk ɔrdər/ (**stock orders**)

MERCHANDISING

NOUN A **stock order** is a request, often created automatically by retail software, for new supplies to refill the inventory and replenish shelves.

○ *Supermarkets are at the forefront of stock order technology, in that the whole process is completely computerized.*

○ *The retailer placed an initial stock order for the new model of just 75 units.*

S

stock|room /stɒkrum/ (**stockrooms**)

MERCHANDISING

NOUN A **stockroom** is a room in which a stock of goods is kept, as in a store or factory.

○ *Stock clerks work in warehouses and stores to guide and maintain the flow of supplies and merchandise in and out of stockrooms.*

○ *The more goods kept, the less space there is in the stockroom for new lines and the more money tied up in the old stock.*

stock|tak|ing /stɒkteɪkɪŋ/

MERCHANDISING

NOUN **Stocktaking** is the process of examining, counting, and valuing goods held by a store or business.

○ *Stocktaking can include the actual counting and weighing of stock.*

○ *If we have some goods on sale or return at the stocktaking date, they should not be included in our stock valuation.*

stock trans|fer /stɒk trænsfər/ (stock transfers)

MERCHANDISING

NOUN **Stock transfer** is the act of moving goods from one part of the distribution chain to another.

○ *An internal purchase order is created for stock transfer between branches and warehouses.*

○ *A traditional stock transfer form should be in triplicate, with one copy held at stock control, one for the warehouse and one to accompany the stock being transferred.*

stor|age u|nit /stɔrɪdʒ yunɪt/ (storage units)

STORE FIXTURES AND LAYOUT

NOUN A **storage unit** is shelving for keeping goods, usually in a warehouse and not on the sales floor.

○ *Refrigerated storage units in the distribution centers store perishables.*

○ *Use storage units with drawers for small items such as socks and ties, so that the sales area is not cluttered.*

store /stɔr/ (stores)

OUTLETS

NOUN A **store** is a business for the retail sale of goods and services.

○ *They plan to open 30 new stores around the country in the next six months.*

○ *Grocery stores and other large retail outlets need an effective distribution system.*

store cred|it /stɔr krɛdɪt/ (**store credits**)

CUSTOMER ACCOUNTS

NOUN A **store credit** is a document offered by a store to a customer who returns an item not eligible for a refund. It can be used to buy other goods at the store.

○ You may exchange merchandise or receive store credit in the amount of the item's last sale price.

○ A merchant normally issues a store credit when a customer returns merchandise that cannot be exchanged.

store front /stɔr frʌnt/ (**store fronts**)

MARKETING

NOUN **Store fronts** are the windows of stores that can be looked into from the street, often displaying the types of product each store sells.

○ Online store fronts should be eye-catching and functional.

○ Store fronts are extremely important as the external appearance of retail stores exerts a big influence on customer attitude.

store|keep|er /stɔrkipər/ (**storekeepers**)

PERSONNEL

NOUN A **storekeeper** is the manager or owner of a store, or a person responsible for managing stores.

○ Storekeepers running mom and pop stores are facing stiff competition from the new shopping mall.

○ The storekeeper receives deliveries and locates them in the storeroom.

S

store launch e|vent /stɔr lɔntʃ ɪvɛnt/ (**store launch events**)

MARKETING

NOUN A **store launch event** is a special event, which publicizes the opening of a new store and at which discounts and free samples may be offered.

○ Come and mingle with the stars at our store launch event in downtown Manhattan.

○ The store launch event is to include fashion shows and free beauty consultations.

store man|ag|er /stɔr mænɪdʒər/ (**store managers**)

PERSONNEL

NOUN A **store manager** is the most senior member of the staff in a store, who is responsible for the overall running of the store.

○ *A grocery store manager needs to be accessible to their staff and customers, so must visit the shop floor regularly.*

○ *The angry customer demanded to see the store manager.*

OTHER STORE MANAGEMENT ROLES

The following are other management roles in a store:

buying manager
a senior employee whose job is to manage the purchase and delivery of products and supplies, maintaining stock levels

operations manager
the person responsible for the store's day-to-day working such as managing stock levels, manpower, display and advertising, and correct pricing

sales manager
a manager responsible for the sales area in a store, including the supervision of sales associates and other employees

security manager
the person responsible for organizing all security in the store and to whom security guards report

---

store re|fur|bish|ment /stɔr rifɜrbɪʃmənt/

STORE FIXTURES AND LAYOUT

NOUN **Store refurbishment** happens when a store needs to be redecorated, modernized or the layout changed. The store will often be closed to customers during this time.

○ *Store refurbishment was carried out in twenty stores to assess the effects of making changes in merchandise, ranges, layout, and design.*

○ *Retailers are watching every penny at the moment – certainly many are cutting back on major store refurbishment programs.*

store roll|out /stɔr roʊlaʊt/ (**store rollouts**)

NOUN **Store rollout** happens when a retailer expands, opening new outlets in a planned way.

○ These stores will use a smaller layout than most furniture stores, providing greater site availability and the opportunity for faster store rollout.

○ Pop-up shops are different, exciting and can be a great way of testing market demand before committing to full-blown store rollout.

strip-mall /strɪp mɔl/ (**strip-malls**)
OUTLETS

NOUN A **strip-mall** is a row of stores trading together in a neighborhood usually providing key local shopping requirements.

○ The main structure of the strip-mall was divided into twenty-six individual retail spaces.

○ Strip-malls at major road intersections can be found in nearly every city or town in the US.

su|per|mar|ket /supərmɑrkɪt/ (**supermarkets**)
OUTLETS

NOUN A **supermarket** is a large self-service retail store selling food and household supplies.

○ The main reason for the decline in the grocer's sales was the competition from several new supermarkets in the area.

○ Supermarkets account for nearly 85% of grocery sales.

RELATED WORDS

Compare **supermarket** with **hypermarket** which is also a self-service store, selling food and household supplies, but is larger and is usually on the outskirts of a town.

su|per|store /ˈsuːpərstɔr/ (superstores)

OUTLETS

NOUN A **superstore** is a very large supermarket, often selling household goods, clothes, and electrical goods, as well as food.

○ *Superstores typically charge anywhere from 15 to 45 percent less than their smaller counterparts.*

○ *The opening of 11 new superstores over the course of six months helped swell the firm's profits to $157 million.*

---

sup|pli|er /səˈplaɪər/ (suppliers)

DISTRIBUTION

NOUN A company's **suppliers** are businesses that supply the company with products or materials.

○ *The company does not make its own products, and thus has no control over manufacturing by its suppliers, who are based in Asia and Europe.*

○ *Some foreign suppliers of raw materials won't release goods until they receive cash payment or a letter of credit from the bank.*

---

sup|ply chain /səˈplaɪ tʃeɪn/

DISTRIBUTION

NOUN The **supply chain** is all of the various stages, in order, of a product's progress from raw materials through production and distribution of the finished product, until it reaches the consumer.

○ *Supply chain management reduces costs by increasing inventory turnover on the shop floor.*

○ *These logistical changes will benefit many companies looking for a shortened supply chain and increased efficiency.*

S

Tt

tag /tæg/ (tags)

NOUN A **tag** is a plastic, fabric, or cardboard label attached to a product, such as a hang tag or security tag.

○ *The tags on the sweaters were attached with small safety pins.*

○ *The price tags on their children's range are cute animal shapes that children like to collect.*

take /teɪk/

NOUN The **take** from a business activity is the profit or money earned from that activity.

○ *He was fairly satisfied with the take from an afternoon's sales.*

○ *The promotion has increased the take for the whole department.*

tak|ings /teɪkɪŋz/

NOUN A store's **takings** is all the money it has been paid for goods in a specified period.

○ *Takings have been down this week because of the wintry weather.*

○ *Each day's takings is transferred to the bank by security van.*

tax /tæks/ (taxes)

COUNT/NONCOUNT NOUN **Tax** is an amount of money that you have to pay to the government so that it can pay for public services such as roads and schools.

○ *The government created a new tax on the retail sale of certain goods and services.*

○ *A retail sales tax is levied on the purchase of a commodity.*

RELATED WORDS

Compare **tax** with **duty** which is a government tax added to the cost of a certain category of goods, such as alcohol, tobacco, or imports and exports.

---

tax re|fund /tæks rifʌnd/ (**tax refunds**)

MANAGEMENT ACCOUNTS

NOUN A **tax refund** is money received back from a tax return.

○ *By recording charitable donations on their tax returns, taxpayers can receive a further tax refund.*

○ *The additional payments will result in either a larger tax refund or a smaller tax bill at the end of the year.*

---

tear|sheet /tɛərʃit/ (**tearsheets**)

MARKETING

NOUN A **tearsheet** is an actual copy of an advertisement, cut from a newspaper or magazine and sent to the retailer as proof of printing.

○ *Each claim must be supported with a full page tearsheet from each newspaper in which the ad ran.*

○ *When a client pays for advertising space in a magazine, someone from the magazine would send the client a tearsheet of the ad as proof of publication.*

---

ten|der /tɛndər/ (**tenders**)

SUPPLIER ACCOUNTS

NOUN A **tender** is an offer to supply goods or services including the price that will be charged.

○ *Contractors should submit tenders in sealed envelopes by 12 noon on Friday.*

○ *The manufacturers all bid for the contract in an open international tender.*

---

terms /tɜrmz/

SUPPLIER ACCOUNTS

NOUN **Terms** are conditions of payment, such as the due date or discount offered for payment within a certain period, usually printed on an invoice.

○ It is not a wise practice to stretch accounts payable to suppliers beyond the payment terms specified on the invoice.

○ The wholesaler is often willing to negotiate terms, especially to secure big orders.

---

thirds /θɜːrdz/

PRODUCTS

NOUN **Thirds** are faulty or damaged goods of a standard lower than seconds.

○ Their products are worse than factory seconds: we call them factory thirds.

○ The crockery on clearance is categorized as seconds, with some thirds, which have more obvious cracks and flaws.

---

tick|et /tɪkɪt/ (tickets)

STORE FIXTURES AND LAYOUT

NOUN A **ticket** is a label attached to merchandise showing the price and other details.

○ Someone had removed the ticket with the product's specifications.

○ Ticket printing can be designed to speed up consumer awareness, create loyalty with a brand, and boost a product's appeal factor.

---

top-of-the-line (in BRIT use **top-end**) /tɒp əv ðə laɪn/

PRODUCTS

ADJECTIVE **Top-of-the-line** products are the best or most expensive products of their kind.

○ The boutique specializes in top-of-the-line luxury goods with little discounting.

○ In Mexico, while big-box retailers are emphasizing everyday low prices, at the other end of the spectrum the number of top-of-the-line outlets is increasing.

---

trade dis|count /treɪd dɪskaʊnt/ (trade discounts)

SUPPLIER ACCOUNTS

NOUN A **trade discount** is an amount by which the price of something is reduced for a person or business in the same trade.

○ People in the construction industry can get trade discounts of up to 50 percent.

○ *We have a number of tradesmen who, although too small to buy directly from the wholesalers, purchase from us at a trade discount.*

trad|er /treɪdər/ (traders)

PERSONNEL

NOUN **Traders** are people who are involved in buying and selling.

○ *The couple are antique traders with a small shop in a local village.*

○ *A number of used car traders have premises in that neighborhood.*

trades|man /treɪdzmən/ (tradesmen)

PERSONNEL

NOUN A **tradesman** is someone who trades, especially a retailer.

○ *Bigger companies get good deals on price and the merchants make their money off the smaller tradesmen.*

○ *The retail chains will take advantage of every opportunity to reach do-it-yourselfers and self-employed tradesmen.*

trades|peo|ple /treɪdzpipᵊl/

PERSONNEL

NOUN **Tradespeople** are people occupied in trade, especially storekeepers.

○ *It is becoming increasingly hard for tradespeople such as barbers and watchmakers to run a profitable business.*

○ *Local tradespeople were amongst the most vociferous objectors to the plans to build a hypermarket.*

trad|ing pe|ri|od /treɪdɪŋ pɪəriəd/ (trading periods)

MANAGEMENT ACCOUNTS

NOUN A **trading period** is a set length of time, usually a number of weeks, months, quarters, or years, in which sales are measured and compared to previous periods.

○ *After a Thanksgiving trading period which was somewhat better than expected, albeit heavily led by discounting, there has been a slump in sales.*

○ *The vital Christmas trading period did not provide many struggling retailers with the lift in volumes they had hoped for.*

traf|fic (in BRIT use **footfall**) /ˈtræfɪk/

GENERAL

NOUN The **traffic** of a shopping mall or store is the number of people who pass through it.

○ *Retailers now have to work much harder at driving traffic into their stores, maintaining their sales volumes, and retaining customer loyalty.*

○ *At trade shows, the name of the game is traffic, as in getting it to your booth.*

trans|ac|tion /trænˈzækʃᵊn/ (**transactions**)

MANAGEMENT ACCOUNTS

NOUN A **transaction** is a piece of business that changes the finances of a company, for example an act of buying or selling something.

○ *Proof of identity is needed, even for a cash transaction.*

○ *The data management system tracks the complete record of every transaction with a customer from the point that their name is entered in its order books.*

turn|o|ver /ˈtɜrnoʊvər/

MANAGEMENT ACCOUNTS

NOUN The **turnover** of stock is the rate at which it is sold and replaced with new stock.

○ *The megastores rely on a high turnover of stock.*

○ *Excess inventory also takes up valuable store or selling space that could be used for items with higher turnover rates and more profit potential.*

turn o|ver /tɜrn ˈoʊvər/ (**turns over, turned over, turning over**)

MANAGEMENT ACCOUNTS

VERB A business **turns over** stock when it replaces the stock it sells with new stock.

○ *Good stock should turn over 2.5 times a year.*

○ *Stock turnover ratio indicates the number of times the stock has been turned over during the period and evaluates the efficiency with which a firm is able to manage its inventory.*

Uu

un|der|buy /ˈʌndərbaɪ/ (underbuys, underbought, underbuying)

VERB When you **underbuy** a product or range of products, you buy less stock than your retail customers want to buy from you.

○ *When you underbuy, sales opportunities are missed.*

○ *When you don't know how much inventory you have on hand, you are apt to either underbuy or overbuy.*

> **WORD BUILDER**
> **under-** = less/not enough
>
> The prefix **under-** often appears in verbs in which there is a sense of doing something less than usual or expected: **underbuy**, **undercharge**, **undercut**, **underprice**.

un|der|charge /ˈʌndərtʃɑrdʒ/ (undercharges, undercharged, undercharging)

TRANSITIVE/INTRANSITIVE VERB If you are **undercharged** for something, you are asked to pay less than its proper price.

○ *When I got home after spending $220 at my local store, I checked the receipt and found they had undercharged me by $25.*

○ *Customers rarely own up when they have been undercharged, but will object loudly when they are overcharged.*

un|der|cut /ˈʌndərkʌt/ (undercuts, undercut, undercutting)

VERB When a business **undercuts** its competitors, it charges less than its competitors to attract customers.

○ *It increases market share with prices that consistently undercut the competition.*

○ *Buying direct from the winery usually means you pay full list price, as they don't want to undercut their wholesale customers.*

---

un|der|price /ˌʌndərpraɪs/ (underprices, underpriced, underpricing)

PRICING

VERB To **underprice** an article for sale is to sell it at too low a price.

○ *Too often, small business owners underprice their goods and services, believing that low prices are the only way they can achieve a competitive advantage.*

○ *Retailers are tempted to underprice their products and services when they enter a new market to ensure its acceptance.*

---

u|nit /yuːnɪt/ (units)

PRODUCTS

NOUN A **unit** is a single item. In retailing, a unit may be a pair of shoes, a bag of sugar, a box of chocolates, a gallon of gas, or a set of golf clubs.

○ *The firm orders the smallest possible number of units with each order.*

○ *The sell-through percentage is the percentage of units sold during a period.*

---

u|nit cost /yuːnɪt kɔst/ (unit costs)

MANAGEMENT ACCOUNTS

NOUN The **unit cost** of a product is the actual cost of making one item.

○ *You may also need to calculate total cost based on unit cost and number of items when you are ordering several items of the same kind.*

○ *The margin for retailers and wholesalers is the difference between the product's selling price and its unit cost.*

---

u|nit price /yuːnɪt praɪs/ (unit prices)

PRICING

NOUN A **unit price** is the price for one item or measurement, such as a pound, a kilogram, or a pint, which can be used to compare the same type of goods sold in varying weights and amounts.

○ *Multiple pricing is selling two or more of the same item at a price that is lower than the unit price of a single item.*

○ *The shelf tag shows the price for the multipack, and the unit price of each can.*

U|P|C /yu pi si/ (short for **universal product code**)

PAYMENT TECHNOLOGY

ABBREVIATION **UPC** is a standard in various countries for creating individual barcodes for retail products.

○ *The last digit of the UPC code is called a check digit and is the far right number on a product package.*

○ *These products have only one UPC number, representing both the single unit (one can of soda) and the multi-unit (a six pack of soda).*

---

use-by date /yuz baɪ deɪt/ (**use-by dates**)

PRODUCTS

NOUN The **use-by date** printed on the packaging of food or other perishables is the last date recommended by the manufacturer or producer on which the product should be eaten or otherwise used.

○ *Each container of food must bear a use-by date.*

○ *The use-by date is not the same as the sell-by date; it is there for customer guidance.*

U|S|P /yu ɛs pi/ (short for **unique selling point, unique selling proposition**)

MARKETING

ABBREVIATION A **USP** is a factor that has been identified as the one that makes a company's product or service different from and better than their competitors.

○ *Your USP showcases the unique advantages or benefits that you offer, in a concentrated compelling way.*

○ *The best way to identify a meaningful USP is to describe the primary benefit your product or service offers customers and then to list other secondary benefits it provides.*

Vv

val|ue /vælyu/

`MARKETING`

NOUN **Value** is the balance between what a customer sees as the benefit to them of a product and the price they have to pay for it.

○ *Good value is what we all want when spending our money on anything.*

○ *The no-frills retailer offers customers very good value for money.*

val|ue re|tail|er /vælyu riteɪlər/ (value retailers)

`OUTLETS`

NOUN A **value retailer** is a retail outlet in which the premises and décor are without frills and where prices are cheaper.

○ *Now, because customers can get low prices almost anywhere, value retailers are not only competing against each other, but against more midmarket retailers.*

○ *The challenge for all value retailers will be maintaining growth and profit levels with such tight margins.*

vend /vɛnd/ (vends, vended, vending)

`GENERAL`

VERB To **vend** is to sell or be sold.

○ *The online retailer vends a range of retro sports apparel.*

○ *The covered market has many small stalls where traders vend locally-made crafts and sweetmeats.*

V

vend|i|ble /vɛndəbᵊl/

`MERCHANDISING`

ADJECTIVE Something that is **vendible** is suitable for, or capable of being, sold or marketed.

○ *The firm specializes in vendible products for beverage machines.*

○ *We need small vendible packs that can be stacked and dropped from our drinks and snack-dispensing machines.*

---

vend|ing ma|chine /vɛndɪŋ məʃin/ (**vending machines**)

`OUTLETS`

NOUN A **vending machine** is a machine from which products are sold. The customer puts money in a slot, selects a product from the menu and the product is dispensed from the machine.

○ *While most vending machines handle only cash transactions, the opposite ratio applies to kiosks which predominantly favor electronic payments.*

○ *Retail vending machines are placed outside the store, allowing customers to purchase items from its collection without having to go into the store.*

---

ven|dor /vɛndər/ (**vendors**)

`PERSONNEL`

NOUN A **vendor** is a company or person that sells a product or service.

○ *The company is struggling with inventory shortages, and faces more problems ahead as vendors say they will supply new merchandise only on a cash basis.*

○ *The company has reduced production costs by following strategies like reducing the number of direct vendors with which it interacts.*

---

ver|ti|cal re|tail|er /vɜrtɪkᵊl ri̱teɪlər/ (**vertical retailers**)

`OUTLETS`

NOUN A **vertical retailer** is a retail business that designs, produces, and sells its own products, without using middlemen or wholesalers, so that it can satisfy customer demands very efficiently.

○ *A vertical retailer tries to own all methods of supplying consumers and to have a retail format that will reach almost every customer.*

○ Vertical retailers, typically selling fashion goods and apparel, control every stage in the supply chain.

V|I|C /viː aɪ siː/ (short for **very important customer**)

MARKETING

ABBREVIATION VIC is a loyalty scheme in the US offering benefits to loyal customers.

○ I needed to treat a VIC to lunch this week, so booked a table at the new sushi restaurant.

○ Time and effort devoted to VICs will produce dividends in increased sales.

---

vir|tu|al re|tail /vɜːtʃuəl riːteɪl/

OUTLETS

NOUN Virtual retail is retailing on the Internet.

○ Many traditional retailers are entering the virtual retail market in support of their physical stores.

○ To enter the virtual retail market, you will need a website, and a reliable means of processing customer payments.

---

vis|u|al mer|chan|dis|ing (ABBR VM) /vɪʒuəl mɜːtʃəndaɪzɪŋ/

MERCHANDISING

NOUN Visual merchandising is the use of attractive displays and floor plans to increase customer numbers and sales volumes.

○ Visual merchandising is the layout of products based on the image they create and how they are "viewed" by the shopper.

○ The new store will include the retailer's latest design concept incorporating irresistible visual merchandising displays aimed at improving the customer's in-store experience.

V

V|M|I /viː ɛm aɪ/ (short for **vendor managed inventory**)

MERCHANDISING

ABBREVIATION VMI is a system in which a seller takes responsibility for an uninterrupted supply of their product to a retailer, so that the retailer will not run out of stock.

○ VMI has gained considerable attention due to the success of third-party vendors who offer added expertise and knowledge that retailers may not possess.

○ In VMI the manufacturer has access to the distributor's inventory data and is responsible for generating purchase orders.

---

vouch|er /ˈvaʊtʃər/ (vouchers)

MARKETING

NOUN A **voucher** is a document showing payment information, or a document that can be presented to receive money.

○ Customers receive a voucher redeemable on their next visit for the difference if our direct competitors are less expensive.

○ If you recommend a friend to our website, you will receive a gift voucher for $20 when they make their first order.

Ww

---

walk-in traf|fic /wɔk ɪn træfɪk/

GENERAL

NOUN The **walk-in traffic** of a store is the number of people who choose to visit it as they pass by.

○ Store retailers use eyecatching point-of-sale material in their windows, designed to generate a high volume of walk-in traffic.

○ Make the most of your walk-in traffic by using mobile technology to alert smartphone users to promotions when they are near your store.

---

ware|house¹ /wɛərhaʊs/ (warehouses)

MERCHANDISING

NOUN A **warehouse** is a large building where goods are stored before they are sold.

○ A pile-up of unsold goods in stores and warehouses is a sign that production is outstripping demand.

○ Where 20 years ago the docks had been lined with dozens of warehouses, there was now one huge container terminal.

> **RELATED WORDS**
>
> Note that in a warehouse, a **bin** is a numbered or coded area which enables stock to be checked and found easily and **storage units** are shelving for keeping goods.

W

---

ware|house² /wɛərhaʊs/ (warehouses)

OUTLETS

NOUN A **warehouse** is a large building, operating either as a storage facility for a chain of stores, or as an independent wholesale business.

○ *The cargo is loaded onto a truck headed for the company warehouse.*

○ *Goods were continuously delivered to the company's warehouses, from where they were selected, re-packed, and dispatched to retail stores.*

---

war|ran|ty /wɒrənti/ (**warranties**)

SERVICE

NOUN If a **warranty** is offered with goods, the buyer is given a written guarantee that the manufacturer or retailer will repair or replace the goods, under certain conditions.

○ *The service contract extended the warranty on the product to two years.*

○ *While we do perform a pressure test to make sure your watch is water resistant, our warranty does not cover water damage.*

> **Talking about warranties**
>
> If a product is **under** warranty, it is protected by a warranty at that particular time.
>
> If something that you do to a product **voids** or **invalidates** a warranty, it means that the warranty is no longer effective.

---

whole|sale¹ /hoʊlseɪl/

GENERAL

NOUN **Wholesale** is the business of buying goods in large quantities from manufacturers or producers and selling smaller quantities to retailers, who will then sell smaller quantities to their customers.

○ *This tends not to be a start-up kind of business, but if retail doesn't appeal to you and you really want to work in the industry, then perhaps wholesale is right for you.*

○ *Within ten years they had built a large and highly profitable wholesale business, selling to the industrial users of electronic equipment.*

W

---

whole|sale² /hoʊlseɪl/

GENERAL

ADVERB Goods bought and sold **wholesale** are bought and sold in large quantities, usually at a cheaper price than retail goods.

○ *The fabrics are sold wholesale to retailers, fashion houses, and other manufacturers.*

○ *If you choose to sell wholesale, first visit potential retailers who might be interested in your products.*

▶ **COLLOCATIONS:**
buy wholesale
sell wholesale

---

whole|sale³ /hoʊlseɪl/

GENERAL

ADJECTIVE A **wholesale** business is a business that sells in large quantities to another business that will resell the items or use them for manufacturing.

○ *The company decided to press its suppliers for lower prices and pass on any wholesale price increases to its customer.*

○ *The company also operates a wholesale business, supplying T-shirts and other casual wear to distributors and screen printers.*

▶ **COLLOCATIONS:**
wholesale business
wholesale price

---

whole|sale⁴ /hoʊlseɪl/ (**wholesales, wholesaled, wholesaling**)

GENERAL

VERB Companies and individuals that **wholesale** products operate wholesale businesses that buy the products from manufacturers and producers and sell them on to retailers.

○ *The company had been wholesaling Christmas trees for some time but switched to retailing them last year when they acquired a new retail outlet.*

○ *The fashion house has signed a distribution deal for its catwalk collections and will now wholesale both its men's and women's ranges, starting next year.*

W

win|dow-dis|play /wɪndoʊ dɪspleɪ/ (**window displays**)

MERCHANDISING

NOUN A **window-display** in a store window shows examples of the goods sold in that store.

○ Next week we will include some budget-friendly ideas for retail shop window displays.

○ Color-coordinated and seasonally themed window displays are the most inviting to shoppers as they pass by.

---

win|dow dress|er /wɪndoʊ drɛsər/ (**window dressers**)

PERSONNEL

NOUN A **window dresser** is a person employed to create attractive displays in store windows.

○ We want to hire a window dresser to help us entice customers into the shop with eye-catching displays.

○ The window dressers often work at night so that the displays will attract shoppers at peak times.

---

win|dow dress|ing /wɪndoʊ drɛsɪŋ/

MERCHANDISING

NOUN **Window dressing** is the design and layout of displays in store windows.

○ A window display of merchandise in a store's window is called window dressing.

○ Thousands of Christmas shoppers are attracted by the store's festive window dressing.

W

Practice
and
Solutions

1. Match the two parts together.

1	BOGO	a	a method of accounting which assumes that the oldest stock is sold first
2	EFTPOS	b	a unique number given to a product so that it can be identified using retail software
3	FIFO	c	the number, known only to you, that you can type into card readers to confirm your identity when paying by credit or debit card
4	LIFO	d	a system for deducting the cost of a purchase direct from the customer's bank, or credit card account by means of a computer link using the telephone network
5	PIN	e	a way of encouraging more sales of a product by offering customers another item of the same type, free or for a reduced price
6	SKU	f	a method of valuing inventory which assumes that the newest stock is sold first

2. Complete the sentences by writing one word or phrase in each gap.

fitting room	store front	shop floor
bargain basement	fascia	checkout counter

1 The .... on a store front is any surface on the outside of the store that displays the company name, logo, and color scheme.

2 A .... in a department store is a floor below the first floor where goods are sold at reduced prices.

3 A .... in a store is a place where customers go to pay for the goods they want to buy.

4 A .... in a store is a cubicle for customers to use when trying on clothes.

5 A .... is the window of a store that can be looked into from the street, often displaying the types of product each store sells.

6 The .... is the area of a store that is accessible by the public, excluding storerooms, stockrooms, and offices.

3. For each question, choose the correct answer.

interiors	apparel	accessories

1 The product category for various types of clothing sold in a store is
....

soft furnishings	haberdashery	home entertainment

2 The product category for items made from fabric such as curtains, cushions, and bedding is ....

nursery	homewares	haberdashery

3 The product category for men's clothing and accessories is
....

| accessories | babywear | nursery |

4 The product category for baby accessories, such as diapers and feeding bottles, is ....

| accessories | interiors | homewares |

5 The product category in fashion stores for items such as scarves, hats, gloves, belts, and purses is ....

| home entertainment | electronic | interiors |

6 The product category for goods and design services for inside the home, including soft furnishings, wall and floor coverings, and lighting is ....

4. Which sentences are correct?

1 Bespoke clothing is made in a series of standard sizes, rather than made to fit the exact measurements of individual customers. ....

2 Seasonal items are available only during certain seasons, or vary with the seasons. ....

3 Top-of-the-line products tend to be fairly cheap compared with other, similar products. ....

4 Niche is used to describe products that appeal to people generally. ....

5 Duty-free goods are exempt from the government tax normally charged on that category of goods. ....

6   Ready-to-wear clothing is made in a series of standard
    sizes, rather than made to fit the exact measurements
    of individual customers.   ....

5. Find the words or phrases that do not belong.

1   Types of store ....
    a vendible   **b** big-box   **c** independent   **d** out-of-town

2   Verbs meaning 'sell' ....
    a vend   **b** retail   **c** invoice   **d** move

3   Types of fixture in a store ....
    a grid merchandiser   **b** gridwall panel   **c** cube unit   **d** cash discount

4   Words related to selling goods cheaply ....
    a apparel   **b** clearance   **c** bargain bin   **d** discount

5   Types of inventory ....
    a perpetual   **b** periodic   **c** physical   **d** peripheral

6   Words referring to big stores ....
    a superstore   **b** flagship store   **c** convenience store
    d department store

6. Put each sentence into the correct order.

1   luxury / brands / carry / all the / both stores
    ....
    ....

2   my PIN / asked / me to / the cashier / enter
    ....
    ....

3 the sales clerk / my change / a twenty-dollar bill / and she gave me /
I gave

....

....

4 the jacket / room to / I went / try on / to the fitting

....

....

5 to giftwrap / I wanted him / the sales clerk / the perfume / asked if

....

....

6 guarantee when / was still under / it stopped / luckily, the radio /
working

....

....

7. Rearrange the letters to find words. Use the definitions to help you.

1 **tursexif**   ....
(in a store, the shelves or shelving units that products are displayed on)

2 **spliday aces**   ....
(an enclosed structure for showing goods, often high-value goods such
as jewelry)

3 **den pac**   ....
(a rack or counter at the end of a store aisle used to display promotional
or sale items)

4 **tengram arck**   ....
(a rail used in stores to hang items of clothing on display, such as shirts
and coats)

5 **drigllaw naple** ....
(a metal grid that can be hung on a wall and used for displaying goods)

6 **walllast pelan** ....
(a slatted surface that can be fixed to the wall from which shelves or
hooks can be hung at varying heights to display merchandise)

8. Match the two parts together.

1 She owns a fancy little boutique

2 The downtown area has lost
most of its independent
retailers and is now

3 Most of these convenience
stores just cannot compete

4 An attractive window display
will bring

5 A concession allows a company

6 People with low incomes will
tend to favor

a with the supermarkets.

b to sell their products inside a
department store that has a
proven client base.

c a lot of walk-in traffic into a
store.

d the discount stores.

e full of chain stores.

f that sells top-of-the-line
designer clothing.

9. Match the two parts together.

1 home

2 bill

3 minimum

4 RFID

5 forwarding

6 drop

a tag

b agent

c shipment

d order

e delivery

f of lading

10. For each question, choose the correct answer.

| rotating stock | stocktaking | stock transfer |

1 The process of examining, counting, and valuing goods held by a store or business is called ....

| stocking unit | stock order | stock transfer |

2 A measurement or number by which items are kept in inventory, for example by dozens, kilograms or cases, is called a

....

| stock allocation | model stock | rotating stock |

3 The decisions made about how quantities held at a central point will be distributed among several outlets in a retail chain is called

....

| stock order | stock allocation | model stock |

4 The maintenance of adequate levels of stock of an item so that enough is always available for selling is called ....

| rotating stock | stock transfer | stock order |

5 The act of moving goods from one part of the distribution chain to another is called ....

| stock order | stockroom | rotating stock |

6 A system used especially in food stores, in which the oldest stock is moved to the front of shelves and new stock is added at the back is called ....

11. Complete the sentences by writing one word in each gap.

underbought	overcharged	undercharged
overstocked	undercut	underpriced

1 The big supermarkets .... smaller convenience stores by as much as thirty or forty per cent.

2 He .... his sports equipment business and is now stuck with a lot of stock on his shelves.

3 I'm sure we .... that product. We could easily have sold it for twenty dollars more.

4 Unfortunately, we .... and didn't have enough ice cream for everyone who came to the stand.

5 I think I've been .... I gave the sales clerk twenty dollars and he only gave me three dollars change.

6 You were .... That should have been thirty dollars and she charged you twenty dollars.

12. Choose the correct word or phrase to fill each gap.

replenishment	turnover	procurement

1 The process of adding more stock to replace what has been sold is called ....

clearance	stocktaking	merchandising

2 The selling of stock, at greatly reduced prices, often to make way for new stock is called ....

destocking	lossmaking	turnover

3 The reduction of the amount of stock held or the ending of holding stock of certain products is called ....

installment	consignment	procurement

4 The act or process of buying stock, including any negotiations that this involves on price and availability is known as

....

assortment	distribution	turnover

5 The rate at which stock is sold and replaced with new stock is called

....

stock order	back order	short order

6 A request, often created automatically by retail software, for new supplies to refill the inventory and replenish shelves is known as a

....

13. Find the words or phrases that do not belong.

1 Words referring to stores selling cheaper products ....
   a discount store   **b** flagship store   **c** value retailer   **d** factory outlet

2 Words referring to someone who buys products or services ....
   a patron   **b** carrier   **c** client   **d** customer

3 Words for people who work on the shop floor ....
   a cashier   **b** cash register   **c** sales associate   **d** sales clerk

4   Words referring to small stores ....
    a emporium   **b** boutique   **c** mom-and-pop store   **d** convenience store

5   Words relating to displaying goods ....
    a window dressing   **b** retail theater   **c** showroom   **d** barcode

6   Types of discount ....
    a trade   **b** category   **c** quantity   **d** cash

14. Rearrange the letters to find words. Use the definitions to help you.

1 **gecahn**   ....
   (the amount of money handed back to a customer when they have paid
   with bills or coins that total more than the amount due)

2 **sach isergtre**   ....
   (a machine on which sales are rung up and recorded, usually with a
   drawer containing money)

3 **maypent**   ....
   (when you give a sum of money in exchange for goods you have
   received)

4 **ipceert**   ....
   (a printed, or sometimes written, statement that shows that you have
   received goods or money)

5 **herovuc**   ....
   (a document showing payment information, or a document that can
   be presented to receive money)

6 **nuderf**   ....
   (the money you have paid for something when it is returned to you)

15. Which sentences are correct?

1 A multiple store is one of several retail enterprises under
the same ownership and management.   ....

2 A retail anchor and a destination store are different terms
for the same thing.   ....

3 A flagship store is the least important store in a chain,
often with the smallest volume of sales.   ....

4 In a department store, a concession is a business with
a license or contract to operate another business within
the store.   ....

5 A cash-and-carry is a self-service retail store.   ....

6 A wholesale business is a business that sells in large
quantities to another business that will resell the items
or use them for manufacturing.   ....

16. For each question, choose the correct answer.

COD	CRM	CVC

1   An abbreviation used to describe payment terms by which cash is paid when goods or services are delivered is ....

FMCG	CRM	FOB

2   An abbreviation used to describe the mix of strategies used by a company to deal with existing customers, or to attract new customers is ....

an MSR	a VIC	a CVC

3   An added security feature on credit cards, in the form of an extra 3 or 4 numbers printed on the back of the card is ....

EFT	EDI	MSR

4   An electronic system that allows a supplier and a retailer to communicate easily is an ....

RTV	MSRP	PVV

5   The number encoded in the magnetic strip on the back of some types of debit or credit cards, which allows the cardholder's PIN to be checked by ATMs and retail card readers is the ....

an RRP	an RTV	a JV

6   An instruction authorizing the return of unwanted or damaged goods to the seller, the cost of which will then be refunded to the buyer, is ....

17. Match the two parts together.

1 processor

2 approval code

3 authorization

4 encryption

5 merchant fees

6 check guarantee

a any system for security and fraud prevention which automatically breaks up and reorders information before it is sent via telephone lines or the Internet

b any method, usually via a plastic card, that guarantees that a payment made by a printed form from a bank will be honored by the account holder's bank

c money charged by a company to a vendor for processing credit card transactions

d a company that deals with payment transactions

e the process of checking that a card holder has enough credit before funds are released to make a payment

f a PIN or other verification sequence of numbers needed to authorize a payment going through the cash register

18. Put each sentence into the correct order.

1 and got / radio back / I took / a refund / the faulty

....

....

2 they carry / I buy my clothes / a wider / there because /
range of brands

....

....

3 the checkout / over ten minutes / waiting in / I spent / line

....

....

4 all their / there was / markdown on / coats and jackets /
a thirty percent

....

....

5 for the living room / a new / ordered online / I've just / pair of curtains

....

....

6 own brand / buy the supermarket's / goods because / I tend to /
they're cheaper

....

....

19. Choose the correct word or phrase to fill each gap.

| floorwalker | operations manager | sales associate |

1 The .... is the person responsible for the store's day-to-day working such as managing stock levels, manpower, display and advertising, and correct pricing.

| An intern | A sales clerk | A shopkeeper |

2 .... is someone, often a young person, employed temporarily for work experience, but usually unpaid.

| category merchandiser | security manager | category planner |

3 A .... is a person whose job is to decide and co-ordinate future inventory and sales volume in one or more product categories.

| store manager | category merchandiser | sales representative |

4 A .... is a person whose job is to maintain stocks, manage displays and promote sales of a certain product category such as footwear.

| floorwalker | sales associate | store manager |

5 A .... is a person who supervises salespersons in a store and advises customers.

| cashier | merchant | personal shopper |

6 A .... is someone who owns or runs a store, or who buys and sells goods for profit.

20. For each question, choose the correct answer.

off	up	out

1 When cashiers and storekeepers add up all the money taken from customers at the end of the working day, they cash ....

through	down	in

2 When a supplier sells a new product to a retail outlet so that the public can buy it, this is known as selling ....

off	out	up

3 To get rid of products left in stock, usually by selling them at very low prices is to sell them ....

off	up	out

4 If a store sells its entire stock, leaving none for customers to buy, it sells ....

over stock	up stock	out stock

5 If a business replaces the stock it sells with new stock, it is said to turn ....

out stock	up stock	over stock

6 If a retailer adds a percentage to its cost to cover its own costs and make a profit, it is said to mark ....

Solutions

Exercise 1

1 **e** a way of encouraging more sales of a product by offering customers another item of the same type, free or for a reduced price

2 **d** a system for deducting the cost of a purchase direct from the customer's bank, or credit card account by means of a computer link using the telephone network

3 **a** a method of accounting which assumes that the oldest stock is sold first

4 **f** a method of valuing inventory which assumes that the newest stock is sold first

5 **c** the number, known only to you, that you can type into card readers to confirm your identity when paying by credit or debit card

6 **b** a unique number given to a product so that it can be identified using retail software

Exercise 2

1 fascia
2 bargain basement
3 checkout counter
4 fitting room
5 store front
6 shop floor

Exercise 3

1 apparel
2 soft furnishings
3 haberdashery
4 nursery
5 accessories
6 interiors

Exercise 4

2 Seasonal items are available only during certain seasons, or vary with the seasons.

5 Duty-free goods are exempt from the government tax normally charged on that category of goods.

6 Ready-to-wear clothing is made in a series of standard sizes, rather than made to fit the exact measurements of individual customers.

Exercise 5

1 **a** vendible
2 **c** invoice
3 **d** cash discount
4 **a** apparel
5 **d** peripheral
6 **c** convenience store

Exercise 6

1 both stores carry all the luxury brands
2 the cashier asked me to enter my PIN
3 I gave the sales clerk a twenty-dollar bill and she gave me my change
4 I went to the fitting room to try on the jacket

5 the sales clerk asked if I wanted him to giftwrap the perfume

6 luckily, the radio was still under guarantee when it stopped working

Exercise 7

1 fixtures
2 display case
3 end cap
4 garment rack
5 gridwall panel
6 slatwall panel

Exercise 8

1 **f** that sells top-of-the-line designer clothing.
2 **e** full of chain stores.
3 **a** with the supermarkets.
4 **c** a lot of walk-in traffic into a store.
5 **b** to sell their products inside a department store that has a proven client base.
6 **d** the discount stores.

Exercise 9

1 **e** delivery
2 **f** of lading
3 **d** order
4 **a** tag
5 **b** agent
6 **c** shipment

Exercise 10

1 stocktaking
2 stocking unit
3 stock allocation
4 model stock
5 stock transfer
6 rotating stock

Exercise 11

1 undercut
2 overstocked
3 underpriced
4 underbought
5 overcharged
6 undercharged

Exercise 12

1 replenishment
2 clearance
3 destocking
4 procurement
5 turnover
6 stock order

Exercise 13

1 **b** flagship store
2 **b** carrier
3 **b** cash register
4 **a** emporium
5 **d** barcode
6 **b** category

Exercise 14

1 change
2 cash register
3 payment
4 receipt
5 voucher
6 refund

Exercise 15

1 A multiple store is one of several retail enterprises under the same ownership and management.
2 A retail anchor and a destination store are different terms for the same thing.

SOLUTIONS SOLUTIONS SOLUTIONS SOLUTIONS SOLUTIONS

4 In a department store, a concession is a business with a license or contract to operate another business within the store.

6 A wholesale business is a business that sells in large quantities to another business that will resell the items or use them for manufacturing.

Exercise 16

1 COD
2 CRM
3 a CVC
4 EDI
5 PVV
6 an RTV

Exercise 17

1 d a company that deals with payment transactions

2 f a PIN or other verification sequence of numbers needed to authorize a payment going through the cash register

3 e the process of checking that a card holder has enough credit before funds are released to make a payment

4 a any system for security and fraud prevention which automatically breaks up and reorders information before it is sent via telephone lines or the Internet

5 c money charged by a company to a vendor for processing credit card transactions

6 b any method, usually via a plastic card, that guarantees that a payment made by a printed form from a bank will be honored by the account holder's bank

Exercise 18

1 I took the faulty radio back and got a refund

2 I buy my clothes there because they carry a wider range of brands

3 I spent over ten minutes waiting in the checkout line

4 there was a thirty percent markdown on all their coats and jackets

5 I've just ordered online a new pair of curtains for the living room

6 I tend to buy the supermarket's own brand goods because they're cheaper

Exercise 19

1 operations manager
2 An intern
3 category planner
4 category merchandiser
5 floorwalker
6 merchant

Exercise 20

1 up
2 in
3 off
4 out
5 over stock
6 up stock

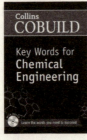

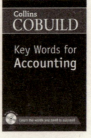
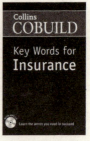
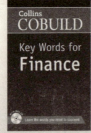

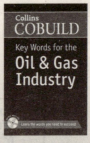